What David Suzuki is to the West Coast, Richard Zurawski is to the East. Richard answers virtually every science question off the top of his head – compelling stuff in live radio situations.
— Andrew Krystal
Host of Maritime Morning
Rogers Maritime Radio

Zurawski presents a rigorous overview of the hows, whys, and what ifs of climate change. His analysis is scientifically based, yet written in clear English – you do not need a science degree to understand the importance of this book and the message it relays. Climate change will likely have significant implications for those of us living close to shore and off the land. All Maritimers would do well to gain a collective understanding of these issues, and this book can help us get there.
— Dr. Edith G.J. Callaghan,
Arthur Irving Academy for the Environment,
Acadia University, Wolfville, Nova Scotia

Richard Zurawski has a gift for making complex scientific concepts understandable and even exciting. In this book, he presents the history of our climate, explains how we are imperilling our future and calls us to action. A must-read book for anyone concerned about the greatest challenge facing the human race.
— Geoff Regan, MP for Halifax West,
Chair of the Liberal Caucus Committee on
Environment and Sustainable Development,
and former federal minister of Fisheries and Oceans

Richard Zurawski has a big brain, a big heart, and a passion for truth-telling about environmental changes. These qualities shine brightly in this fascinating volume. It is a book that exhibits that rare combination of extensive knowledge, deep insight, and wonderful readability. It will be a breakthrough read for those who feel overwhelmed by the issue of global warming and its many studies. For those of us who live in the Maritimes, it is an indispensable description of what we will experience and what we are called to do.
— Dr. Russell Daye
Senior Minister, St. Andrew's United Church, H~~alif~~

D1508782

The Maritime Book
of
Climate Change

Richard Zurawski

Pottersfield Press, Lawrencetown Beach, Nova Scotia, Canada

Library and Archives Canada Cataloguing in Publication

Zurawski, Richard

The Maritime book of climate change / Richard Zurawski.

ISBN 978-1-895900-97-2

1. Climatic changes--Atlantic Provinces. I. Title.

QC985.5.M37Z865 2008   551.5'253   C2008-900217-2

Cover design by Gail LeBlanc

Graphics and illustrations by Rob MacDonald

Cover and interior photos by Richard Zurawski

Pottersfield Press acknowledges the financial support of the Government of Canada through the Book Publishing Industry Development Program for our publishing activities. We also acknowledge the support of the Canada Council for the Arts for our publishing program. We thank the Province of Nova Scotia for its support through the Department of Tourism, Culture and Heritage.

Pottersfield Press
83 Leslie Road
East Lawrencetown, Nova Scotia, Canada, B2Z 1P8
Website: www.pottersfieldpress.com
To order phone toll-free 1-800-NIMBUS9 (1-800-646-2879)
Printed in Canada

This book is dedicated to all the people of the Maritimes
who have opened their hearts and
accepted me as a Maritimer
these past two decades
and
to my teachers at the University of Windsor,
especially Professors Om Chandna,
Mordechay Schlesinger, John McConkey
and Reinhard Helbing,
who had confidence and faith in me
and who inspired and guided me
all those years ago
when I was an undergraduate for a second time.

Contents

Chapter 5
Acting – Private, Government and Individual

Chapter 6
The Future Weather and Climate
of the Maritimes

An Introduction to the
Weather and Climate of
Yesterday, Today and Tomorrow

Whether we like it or not, climate change is a reality. It is all too apparent that we will have to face the folly of our unrestricted growth, consumption and population. If we are to come to grips with the coming changes we will have to learn to rein in some basic human traits. This is truly a war against ourselves and to quote Pogo, Walt Kelly's comic strip possum from the Okeefenokee Swamp, "We have met the enemy and he is us."

Changes and Constants

We live in a time of incredibly stable and consistent climate. The climate of the past 5,000 years has been by and large free of dramatic and destructive swings in weather patterns. But this has not been true of the longer term. In general, the climate and weather of the distant past has tended to be more unstable, variable and even dangerous. We have benefitted enormously from these relatively recent benign weather patterns and have been lulled to think the climate as we know it is a normal pattern. Unfortunately, we are in for a surprise. Scientists tell us it is unlikely, under any circumstances, that we can expect the climate to be as stable as it has been these past few millennia. We are at a cusp of change, in part due to the natural change in climate because of the cyclical nature of ice ages we are currently in and in part due to humanity's influence on the weather and climate patterns. Both effects are capable of producing rapid and sudden climate change and influencing one another in ways that are not totally understood. What is understood, is that by adding the human-induced climate change element to the weather equation, we almost surely are creating a pattern that will sooner rather than later bring more frequent and more violent weather.

Richard B. Alley tells us in his book, *The Two-Mile Time Machine: Ice Cores, Abrupt Climate Change, and Our Future*, that the two-mile-long ice core extracted from the Greenland ice cap indicates that large, rapid climate and weather fluctuations have been the norm rather than the exception and that onset of a major shift in climate, either cooling or warming, takes just a few years. This amazing ice core represents just over 100,000 years of climate record.

In the Maritimes, the climate has come a long way in a short time. Twelve thousand years ago glaciers three kilometres thick covered the region. Evidence of the ice advance can be seen in the erratics, rocks deposited by the retreating glaciers and stranded in places like Peggy's Cove, and the thin soil along the South and Eastern Shores of Nova Scotia. As recently as 100 years ago winters were longer and cooler.

But it wasn't always cooler. About 1,000 years ago the Norse crossed the Atlantic to colonize North America. The Medieval Warm Period from 800 to 1400 led to ocean voyages of exploration by many cultures in Europe and Asia. New evidence tells us that not only the Norse and Basques had trekked to the Maritimes, but the Chinese may have journeyed here too. Paul Chaisson's *The Island of Seven Cities: Where the Chinese settled when they discovered America* explores the possibility that the great Chinese expedition of 1421 may have visited Cape Breton.

Despite its oscillations, the climate has been for the most part benevolent. But now most scientists who study weather and climate agree there are additional changes happening and these changes will be larger and faster than any that have happened at any time in the more than 12,000 years since the last glacial retreat. What's more, the coming changes, their intensity and the degree of their variation are something that we humans are going to have to accept the blame for. Through our total domination of our ecosystem we are affecting a dramatic and potentially catastrophic climate change. And once the climate genie is out of the bottle, there will be hell to pay because, it appears from past records, that when the climate changes, the changes are fast and furious. The weather swings are severe and harder to predict.

Our extensive peat bogs are wonderful repositories of climate information. Because organic material is largely preserved in the anaerobic bogs, researchers have collected detailed samples that help them identify the plants that grew in the Maritimes since the last ice advance. Seeds, insects and leaves are all preserved in the bogs and by comparing these samples with existing plants and animals we can track the differences and similarities in climate. Our peat bogs contain species of plant and animal that have long since disappeared in the region because of the changing climate. In England, human bodies, some over 2,000 years old, have been found in bogs. The preservation of the anaerobic environment is so good that facial features, hair, skin and muscle tissue are still intact and identifiable.

We have only been keeping detailed records of the weather and climate for a little more than 150 years. To go back farther to see trends that existed before then, we have had to be creative in our collection and interpretation of data. Pollen samples from ancient lake beds, ice core samples from the Antarctic and Arctic, glacial till (the soil, gravel and sand left behind by the retreating glaciers) and sediment deposited on ocean bottoms through the ages all have within them the information that we seek. All tell us something of the climate record and all have been used to extract information about the weather and the climate of the past (paleoclimate). It has only been in the past few decades that we have been able to create an accurate, comprehensive climate story from information gleaned from many sources.

Though we have had many indications and much evidence pointing to the fact that human activity could be, and in all probability is, responsible for a climate shift, we have been reluctant as a population to accept the facts and endorse a change in our consuming habits.

In the past 10,000 years of human ascension, from just a few million souls clinging to life in a post-ice age peak, to a world covered in our sprawling billions and scarred by our industry, Greenpeace estimates that we have consumed more than 50 percent of our planet's resources through overfishing, agribusiness, species extinction and reduction of natural ecosystems.

Species Extinction Rate: The rate of extinction of species over the past 10,000 years is estimated to be comparable to the rates of the five major mass extinctions of the Phanerozoic Eon or last 545 million years. They occurred during the Ordovician, Devonian, Permian, Triassic and most famously, the Cretaceous periods. The last, the Cretaceous extinction, ended the reign of dinosaurs 65 million years ago.

In the Maritimes the species that have disappeared or virtually disappeared include black bears, cougars, lynxes, wolves, woodland caribou, martins, fishers and peregrine falcons, just to name a few. Thousands of species of birds, plants, insects and fish will disappear in the decades to come if current trends continue.

As we convert the planet's resources to satisfy our own needs, we have run afoul of the natural balance of life. We have been able to change the world to suit our needs in such a dramatic and profound way that every other species is subordinate to and dependent on us for its survival. Our needs and wants have intruded on land, water and air to such an extent that the ecosystem, and specifically the climate that gave rise to us and our civilization, the stable, predictable weather, is now on the cusp of massive change.

In the Maritimes we have a long list of minerals that we extract from the Earth, in addition to our propensity for logging and fishing, which also destroys the habitats of creatures with whom we used to coexist. Coal is foremost on that list. Mines have been operating in Nova Scotia and New Brunswick for hundreds of years and coal has been the major source of power in Nova Scotia.

The Energy Accounts for The Nova Scotia Genuine Progress Index, a 2004 report by the not-for-profit group GPI (Genuine Progress Index) Atlantic, estimated the total damage costs resulting from air pollutant and greenhouse gas emissions attributable to energy use in Nova Scotia in 2000 to be between $617 million and $4 billion, depending on assumptions and methodologies used. That averages out to $1.6 billion a year.

As we digest the stacks of information and try to understand the underlying causes and effects, we are finding that we can no longer treat the resources and the atmosphere of the planet as an infinite space far beyond our feeble reach. Our technology has allowed us to exceed our wildest dreams. As we churn the natural ecosystem into consumables to satisfy our every want, we also exert a pressure against the natural balance that has held sway for all these wonderfully benevolent centuries.

One of the inescapable facts gleaned from the mounds of

paleoclimate data that cannot be overlooked is the direct relationship between CO_2 (carbon dioxide) and average global temperature. Data from Antarctic ice cores, published in *Nature* magazine in 1999 by J.R. Petit and his colleagues, correlate CO_2 bubbles trapped in the ice with global air temperature and detail 420,000 years of interlocked CO_2 and global air temperature. This provides a stunning, graphical representation of how closely the two mesh. Higher CO_2 levels are locked to higher global temperatures. Lower CO_2 levels mean cooler temperatures.

Whether you want to believe that this is true or not, this is the evidence and it is irrefutable. What caused the higher CO_2 levels is now what scientists are trying to figure out.

Total greenhouse gas (GHG) emissions for Nova Scotia in 1997 were 20 million tonnes, an increase of 3 percent over the 1990 amount of 19.4 million tonnes. Reliable recent figures for total GHG emissions are difficult to obtain, but groups like PollutionWatch, Clean Nova Scotia, and the Ecology Action Centre estimate from various studies that current GHG emissions in Nova Scotia are close to 23 million tonnes per year.

Prince Edward Island emits just over two million tonnes and New Brunswick 24 million tonnes of CO_2 and other GHGs, according to the Environment Canada Greenhouse Gas Summary website. The IPCC – the United Nations Intergovernmental Panel on Climate and Change – reported in 2008 that the national average in Canada was 21 tonnes per person per year. While Prince Edward Island and New Brunswick were below the national average, their GHG contributions were at least ten times higher than the global average of two tonnes per person.

Since the onset of the latest round of ice ages, some three million years, the ice has advanced and retreated on average every 100,000 to 150,000 years, somewhere between fifteen and twenty times. In essence, the past 110,000 years is just a tiny snapshot of the entire ice age.

No credible scientist today doubts that we are in the midst of a cycle of ice boom and bust, that the ice has advanced and retreated many times over the past three million years, during the current ice ages. The questions we have to ask are, what can this tell us about what is happening now and what makes this round different from all the others?

It is unlikely that this cycle is any different from the many that have preceded it. The last advance and retreat, taking place over the past 110,000 years, appears quite similar to the twenty or so that have happened in the past. And it appears that the current ice age cycle will have many, many more cycles and will last many more millions of years. As long as there is no significant change in the distribution of the Earth's continents we will be locked into the current ice age cycles.

> So much water was tied up in glaciers at the height of the last ice advance that the ocean levels were as much as 120 metres lower than they are today. That means Nova Scotia, New Brunswick and Prince Edward Island had land areas 30 percent larger than they are today, the Bay of Fundy did not exist, and PEI was connected to the mainland, as was Newfoundland. But it would have been hard to call this land since all this area was covered in ice two kilometres thick. This was only 12,000 years ago and is expected to happen again and again in the millennia to come.

Right now we are at the height of an interglacial, the time between the major advances of ice. On average, these interglacial periods last about 10,000 years, while the ice advances last ten times as long. Already this interglacial has lasted slightly longer than the average and it is expected that soon, over the next few centuries, we are going to have a major shift into the next great ice advance. But there is a caveat in this – human activity. If it weren't for human activities, the CO_2 levels would begin to fall, most probably being absorbed by the increased volume and surface area of the world's oceans, because of the massive global ice melt.

Our activities are adding incredible amounts of CO_2 to the atmosphere at a stunningly prodigious rate. How much? The atmosphere contains almost 1,000 billion tonnes of carbon, almost all of it in the form of carbon dioxide. That amount is rising and a significant fraction, about one-third, is directly attributable to human activity. How fast is the CO_2 rising? A decade ago the rate of CO_2 increase was 1.8 to 2 parts per million. At the Mauna Loa Climate Observatory in Hawaii in 2004 the levels were measured to be 380 parts per million and increasing at a rate of 3 parts per million per year and accelerating.

According to the IPCC (Intergovernmental Panel on Climate and Change), Canada's greenhouse gas emissions (per capita) have the dubious distinction of being among the highest in the world. Nova Scotia is among the highest in Canada, with Green Energy making up less than 1 percent of the total of the entire energy grid in the Maritimes. New Brunswick is slightly higher in GHG emissions than Nova Scotia and PEI is below the national average.

In 2004 PEI generated 0.5 percent of its electricity from on-Island wind power, but in 2007 had increased that to 15 percent through new wind turbines. New Brunswick and Nova Scotia have yet to make that kind of breakthrough using renewable energy.

In 50 years the CO_2 content could be double what it is today. In comparison, at the height of all the interglacials, the

CO_2 levels were never higher than 300 parts per million. We are clearly entering into uncharted waters and what it means for the climate patterns, the current cycle of ice ages, the weather conditions, and for the world in general is in the realm of speculation. In fact, to find a time in the Earth's history when CO_2 levels are anywhere as high as what we fear they will reach in the coming decades, we have to go back tens or even hundreds of millions of years.

Today there is a great debate as to what these higher levels of CO_2 will mean over the coming decades. One of the arguments by those opposed to the view that we are creating an untenable situation with our increased economic and industrial output is that if we cannot even forecast the weather more than two weeks in advance, how can we even entertain any modelling of the coming years, decades and centuries.

There is a very simple answer to this question. Climate prediction is not the same as weather prediction. Climate is the pattern of weather. For instance, we say that in the northern hemisphere, it is colder in the winter months and hotter during the summer. This is not weather prediction, but it does say what the trends are. We would expect that in most areas of Canada the climate would be cold enough during the winter that we would have snow and that during the summer there would be liquid precipitation in most areas.

Nova Scotia and New Brunswick have some of the world's great institutes for studying the environment, most notably the Bedford Institute of Oceanography (the largest oceanographic institute in Canada) and St. Andrew's Biological Station (the oldest in Canada). Yet over the years government funding has been decreased to the point where many of the world-class researchers have left for greener pastures. In May 2006, Canada's Conservative government slashed funds designed to cut GHGs, leading groups like the David Suzuki Foundation to say that "Canada doesn't have a climate change program anymore."

What climatologists are warning us about is that as CO_2 levels climb and rocket past what we have had in previous times, the weather patterns and the general climate of the Earth is going to warm. The stable climate that we have come to rely on and expect is threatened. The latest models are now creating climate scenarios that should concern us all.

> It is an irony that the Maritimes, which receive very healthy amounts of precipitation, could experience drought because of climate change. Due to decreased snowfall, longer summers and increasing numbers of severe storms, rain and snow-melt run off very quickly and are less likely to be absorbed in the underground water table. Increased threat of forest fires, lower agricultural yields and wells drying up are a result of climate change.

In Canada, many would argue a warmer climate would be a great benefit and boon to us. But it is not as simple as that. Global warming doesn't mean that all areas will get a bit warmer and more like the southern havens that many Canadians seek during the winter months in Florida and California. Global warming also means increased numbers and severity of storms, species extinction, changes in precipitation amounts and patterns, and above all a decrease in the global ice caps in Greenland and Antarctica. The melting of the ice caps means more water, changes in salinity, higher ocean levels, and modified ocean currents. In short, it affects the energy transfer of the world's mightiest power transfer system.

Global warming in its simplest and most general terms is about energy input into a basically closed system. Increased levels of CO_2 in the atmosphere is just another way of saying the Earth is retaining more of the heat it receives from the sun. If we didn't have an atmosphere that could retain the heat and distribute it across the surface of the Earth, then we would have a surface that would be excruciatingly hot in the daylight hours and frigid during the night. The greenhouse effect moderates the extremes, by retaining much of the daylight heat and keeping it trapped for the night hours. The process of heat distribution is what makes the Earth's ecosystem unique. Heat storage and release mechanisms have kept the Earth and its climate in a comfortable range for life for almost four billion years. James Lovelock coined a phrase for this, the Goldilocks Effect.

Some amount of greenhouse effect is necessary for the Earth to be a comfortable place. But as in most circumstances, too much of a good thing is not good. We are entering the realm of uncertainty because there is just too much of a good thing.

The Gulf Stream – Ocean Conveyor

The Gulf Stream current transfers massive amounts of heat from the tropics to the more temperate regions to the north. This gives the Maritime provinces the moderation we have come to rely on for the past thousand years.

As the climate warms, the global ice caps accelerate their melt and in the case of Greenland, the melt increases to such an extent that it upsets the North Atlantic salinity profile because the melt is fresh water. The east coast of North America and Europe rely on a warm ocean stream, the Gulf Stream, which is part of the Ocean Conveyor, to transfer the warmth of the tropics to our northern climes.

The Gulf Stream is propelled by the sinking of cold, salty (and therefore denser) waters in the North Atlantic Ocean. That creates a void that pulls warm, salty surface waters northward. The ocean gives up its heat to the atmosphere above the North Atlantic, and prevailing winds carry the heat eastward to warm Europe.

The worry is that if too much fresh water from the Greenland ice cap enters the North Atlantic, its waters could stop sink-

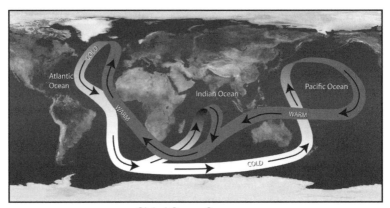

Global Ocean Conveyor.

ing and the pull on the warm waters would end. The conveyor would slow or, in a worst case scenario, cease. Heat-bearing Gulf Stream waters would no longer flow into the North Atlantic, and European and North American winters would become more severe. All this would happen as the rest of the world would continue to heat up under global warming.

Here is the problem. As the Greenland melt accelerates and puts ever increasing amounts of fresh water into the North Atlantic, the flow of the stream is being interrupted. Over the past two decades, it has been determined that the Gulf Stream has declined by almost 30 percent.

> More than any other place in North America, the Maritimes and Atlantic Canada would bear the brunt of a change to the global conveyor. Increased iceberg activity, longer and more severe winters as well as a shorter summer season would all make life more difficult, not to mention much cooler.

By adding new variables to the weather and climate equations, we have also added a great instability to the understanding of the weather patterns and climate that we have come to rely on. It is the unpredictable change that we must now worry about.

End of the Interglacial

The flip from the warm interglacial that we are now experiencing to a new ice advance is inevitable. We know that from the great past records, from ice core samples, ice scars, glacial tills, glacial scouring (what happens when the glaciers scrape the soil off the bedrock), and a host of other evidence. If we could discount the effects of people and their activities, then it is almost certain what happened during the past twenty or so cycles of glacial advance and retreat would once again be repeated. And probably within a thousand years, give or take a couple of centuries.

But we have intervened and it appears that all bets are off. We have added a huge amount of new greenhouse gases and we don't know how bad, sudden or intense the changes will be. But we know there will be changes and based on what has happened in the past, the changes will tend to be rapid. More alarmingly, once they happen the conditions will not reverse for many years, perhaps even centuries, until the trends again reach a tipping point that reestablishes a more benevolent climate regime.

In the past 13,000 years, within the overall context of a global warming trend, as the Earth entered its latest interglacial, there were four events – three of them rather dramatic coolings – that presented major challenges to humanity:

> • The Younger Dryas, a dramatic cooling 12,700 years ago where the average temperatures in the North Atlantic region abruptly plummeted by nearly five degrees Celsius and stayed that way for 1,300 years before rapidly warming again.

- The 8,200-Year Event was similar to the Younger Dryas, but not so severe and of shorter duration, only about a century.

- The Medieval Warm Period, an abrupt warming that took place about 1,000 years ago. It was not nearly so dramatic as the previous two coolings, but nonetheless allowed the Norse to establish colonies and settlements in Greenland.

- The Little Ice Age occurred between 1300 and 1850, where the climate turned abruptly colder. It had profound agricultural, economic and cultural impacts in Europe and was the cause of the Norse abandoning many of their northern settlements, most notably in Greenland.

These four events illustrate that our climate has changed dramatically in a short time and that the changes lasted for prolonged periods before settling back into the general trend. This tells us that dramatic change is a part of the overall normality of the climate. In addition, despite the fact that for the past 13,000 years we have been in a state of warming, an interglacial, three of these dramatic climate changes were coolings. This also tells us that even though the general trend of the climate may be one of warming, there have been occurrences where the changes have gone against the trend.

Computers and Information

The new information over the past decade from researchers investgating the ocean-atmosphere interface is that we are on the threshold of another major climate change. And again, it may well be that the land area bounding the North Atlantic, northern

Europe and North America, which is dependent on the warmth of the Gulf Stream, may be in for a major cooling shift while the rest of the world continues to warm under the increased greenhouse gas effect.

Researchers are spending more time and effort studying the critical and very important ocean-atmosphere connection. With the advent of nano and satellite technology we can now collect vast amounts of information from very sophisticated satellites and process it with incredibly powerful models. And what these models are pointing out seems to agree very well with what has happened in the past.

> The Maritime Weather Office in Halifax, Nova Scotia, is the climate and weather forecast centre for the Maritime provinces as well as the home of the Canadian Hurricane Centre. The CHC provides severe storm information and forecasting for the Maritimes and conducts research into the nature, movement and life cycles of all sorts of severe weather ranging from hurricanes to extratropical storms to nor'easters. Their studies include data on wind speed, wave heights, storm duration, storm energy sources and system extent. The CHC is one of two centres in North America for the monitoring and forecasting of Atlantic hurricanes – the other is the National Hurricane Center in Miami, Florida – and the only centre to specialize in Extratropical Disturbances.

Less conjecture and more science is coming out of the studies. This is what the researchers have found. What makes climate change different now from past times is people. In the past the movers and shakers of the dramatic climate shift came from nature. This time around climate change is occurring because of the action of each one of us. Where it will lead us is the scary part, because no one has the answers, since this has never happened before.

The Great Dying

It seems that as far as the climate is concerned everything is interrelated and linked. There is a real danger we may be inducing what is called a runaway greenhouse effect, where we set the climate on an uncharted path by adding so much greenhouse gases (GHG) to the atmosphere that it becomes a positive feedback loop.

A positive feedback loop is a system that once started continues to accelerate all by itself. The climate will then continue on a warming trend until it has established a new and much higher average global temperature. If we continue to pump GHGs into the atmosphere, scientists are afraid that this new temperature may be almost 25 degrees warmer than anything we have experienced in the last quarter of a billion years. If that happens most life will certainly find the conditions unbearable.

Has this ever happened in the past to give us a precedent for this kind of thinking? It appears that it may have happened a long time ago.

The greatest mass extinction in the last half billion years occurred 251 million years ago – the Permian Mass Extinction or the Great Dying. It was so great that 95 percent of all living species died out. In the space of what may have been as long as a million years or as short as a few thousand, changes in the climate were set in place that had drastic consequences for the life on Earth at that time.

Recent studies into the causes of this massive calamity indicate a number of things happened that resonate with our current state of affairs.

For some reason it appears that the average temperature of Earth rose to unprecedented levels. Some estimates show average temperatures at over 40°C. This caused changes in the ocean, massive oxygen deletion, which led to huge dead zones called anoxic regions. The global climate took thousands and thousands of years to return to cooler conditions and for carbon dioxide and other greenhouse gases to stabilize to their pre-disaster levels.

To determine the reasons for the Great Dying, we have to take into account the placement of the Earth's continents, which were vastly different from what we see today. What makes the continents shift over time is something scientists call plate tectonics. It has been and will continue to be active, moving the continents across the face of the earth with dramatic results.

The inner Earth is molten because of radioactive elements which provide heat. This heat makes the interior molten and fluid. Its ebbing and flowing drives the movement of the crustal plates. The movement is ever so slow, but if you have the time, millions upon millions of years, the changes are incredible. At the time of the Great Dying, there was only one continent and one ocean, because all the continents were smashed together in one vast land mass called Pangaea, surrounded by one huge ocean called Panthalassa. Pangaea stretched from almost the South Pole to the North Pole, with massive, almost endless deserts and huge mountain ranges. Pangaea lasted almost 100 million years before plate tectonics began to rift the massive continent apart.

Ocean currents were able to carry energy from the equator to the poles, affecting climate and weather dramatically. Stating exactly what it must have been like and what seasons the Earth had at that time is still well within the realm of speculation, though paleoclimatologists (scientists who study climates of the past and past climate changes) are now closer than ever to being able to tell us. More research and collection of data in remote areas that were formerly inaccessible as well as computer aided parsing of old and new information are yielding results.

Most of Pangaea's interior is thought to have been a near desert and because there was no great land mass over either pole, no great ice caps formed. Through most of the Carboniferous and Permian Periods the global climate was warmer than today's.

During the Carboniferous and Permian Periods, the climate of the Maritimes was subtropical to tropical, similar to what is found in southern Florida and the Caribbean islands today. The plants and animals were nonflowering and cold-blooded (exothermic).

In the fossil cliffs of Joggins, Nova Scotia, there is evidence of the vast cycad forests, a type of seed plant that is today a small component of the plant kingdom and only found in tropical and subtropical regions. In addition to the cycads and ferns, we can find a myriad of fossilized amphibians, insects and arthropods that scurried about on the forest floor.

Joggins is being considered as a World Heritage Site because of its spectacular fossil cliffs, which date from the Carboniferous to Triassic Periods. During that time the Maritimes were sandwiched on the continent of Pangaea between North America, Africa and Asia, and on the shores of the mega ocean called Panthalassa.

Giant fossilized cycads in Joggins cliffs.

Fossilized trilobite from Joggins.

Changes

Australia, the driest and most desertified continent in the world, is suffering from the worst drought in its recorded history. Climatologists have dubbed it "the one in a thousand year drought" and it shows no signs of abating. The two largest and most important river systems, the Murray and Darling, have been reduced to mere trickles and many of the farms and ranches in the outback are suffering from incredibly arid conditions. Once one of the largest wheat producers in the world, Australia's output, on which much of Asia depends, has been drastically reduced and today, though self-sufficient, Australia's agricultural capacity continues to fall.

While our concerns in the Maritimes are about too much water, ice and increased frequency and intensity of storms, Australia is the poster child for the arid aspect of global warming, something that also concerns the interior of North America. Already the Ogallala Aquifer (also known as the High Plains Aquifer) – the vast underground lake found under the states of South Dakota, Nebraska, Kansas, Oklahoma, Texas, Wyoming, Colorado and New Mexico – has had its levels drastically lowered because of intensive agricultural irrigation brought on by low rainfall amounts and high evaporation rates. It waters one-fifth or 20 percent of US irrigated land. It is vast but shallow and only restocked by snowmelt and rainfall, which is much less than the yearly drain due to irrigation. Already the encroachment of the southern deserts of Arizona, Nevada and Utah are being felt throughout the southwest.

It doesn't take much of a change in rainfall to dramatically affect a region. Even the type of rainfall and snowfall can have long-lasting and sweeping effects. In the Maritimes storms are becoming more frequent and severe. Continuous periods of precipitation are becoming less frequent. Even though there isn't much change in rainfall totals, what does fall comes in shorter, more severe bursts, giving heavier rains which wash out, flood and damage the ground. Less water is soaked into the ground and as a result, water tables become lower; plants with shorter and less extensive root structures die or are blown over by the more severe winds. What soil does accumulate is washed and swept away, leaving it harder for surviving plants to maintain a hold.

All these effects have been noticed in the Maritimes over the past few decades as the climate has shifted. And while we don't have a drought of the proportions of that in Australia or parts of Africa, many wells are now going dry during the winter and droughts have become more significant in agricultural and rural regions.

Lower snowfall amounts from milder winters means less water for the water table and more evaporation from lakes. Many lakes in Kejimukjik Park, Nova Scotia, are at their lowest levels in decades.

Forest fires in New Brunswick have taken a greater toll with each passing season as the climate changes. Wetlands are becoming drier, and plants and animals are all affected as the rainfall and snowfall patterns begin to shift.

It is surprising to think that the changes in our Maritime climate may trigger an ice age and at the same time be related to increased temperatures and aridity in parts of the world far removed from us. The huge global population and the environmental influence it has are changing the climate and the weather around us. And much of the change is surprising in its rapidity, complexity and intensity.

The next few chapters are about these changes, their causes and the effects, and what we in the Maritimes can expect over the coming decades. Nothing in this world happens in isolation any more. Everything is linked and has an effect. And sadly, we will come to learn this the hard way. In truth, now that we have set this all in motion, the task has become harder. If we had instituted changes in consumption and GHG emissions even a few years ago it would have softened the climate change effects. If we are to mitigate to any degree the changes and the intensity of the changes that will befall us we have to act now, and act in substantial ways that dramatically lower the gases we put into the atmosphere. We must consider everything and make changes to energy consumption, population and our economic models.

The sooner we begin to realize that we have to end the effluent we pour into the ecosystem, the greater the chance that we and our biosphere will survive. The worst case is that we don't, that we continue on with a business as usual attitude and measure our world in terms of dollars and cents and what we can wring out of it for our own short-sighted interests. In this awful case, tens – possibly hundreds – of millions of people and countless species will suffer and die as the climate settles into a new equilibrium for the next thousand years.

1

Movers and Shakers in Weather and Climate

The climate and weather of the Earth is an awfully complicated system involving the motions and energy of billions and billions and billions of individual particles. There is so much information to be processed that creating the weather forecast requires the world's most powerful computers. But, on the other hand, what drives the weather is enormously simple.

A number of key factors are measured and used to create a forecast. They are wind velocity, temperature, barometric pressure and humidity, to name just a few. But none of these makes the weather. They are just components of the weather. There is really only one prime mover that creates the conditions we measure: heat. And almost all the heat that affects the Earth's ocean-air ecosystem comes from the sun. It's surprising how simple it is. It's very similar to accounting, but instead of money in and out, in the atmosphere, it's heat in and heat out. Physicists call this movement of heat from one place to another thermodynamics. Ultimately, by measuring barometric pressure, temperature and all the other factors of the air, we are measuring the energy and monitoring the effects of the flow of heat in the dynamic ocean-atmosphere interface.

The Earth has, using some pretty basic arithmetic, about 4.3 billion cubic kilometres of air atmosphere. Sounds like a lot, doesn't it? But, really, considering our huge population, our global industry and the fact that there are about ten million other species all sharing the same space, we get an entirely different picture.

If we say that right now there are six billion people on the face of the Earth (we are adding about 90 million new people a year so setting an exact population is difficult), that means each and every person has about 1.5 cubic kilometres of air. That is a parcel of air one kilometre wide by one kilometre long by 500 metres thick.

That parcel has to sustain and include, per person, all the factories, heating, travel and home effluent, remain pure enough to breathe for the entire life of a person and include all the atmospheric sustenance for every living plant, animal, fungus and microbe on Earth. Fly over any urban expanse and you get an idea of how pervasive human activity is. Even agriculture is not without its impact on the atmosphere, land and water.

In the Maritimes we have a total population of roughly two million and a land area just under 150,000 square kilometres, giving a ratio of about fifteen people per square kilometre.

The Differences Between Air Pollution, Smog and Global Warming Gases

Not all pollutants are created equal, nor are their effects interchangeable.

Human activity now covers the earth. We now live in a world where there is no place without air pollution or its effects. Even places that were once considered to be pristine and too far from the centres of human activity have become tarnished with our airborne effluent.

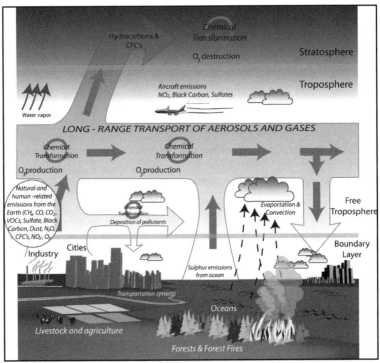

Smog, air pollution and cycles of various gases and pollutants.

In the high Arctic it was common in the 1950s for weather observers to report horizontal atmospheric visibilities of 300 kilometres. Today it is rare that visibilities are 50 kilometres. Particulate matter from industry has circled the globe. Evidence of it can be found not only in the visibility of the air, but also in the snow and rain that falls to Earth and in our lakes, rivers, streams and oceans.

Air pollution is basically anything that is put into the air by industry, people and our activities. This is a blanket category that includes smog, exhaust, all gases that come from industry, including carbon dioxide, and tiny soot and ash particles. In general, air pollution is anything that is found in the air that doesn't belong there and that has the potential to be harmful to life.

Sometimes air pollution comes from natural sources, like outgassing of volcanoes and forest fires. But, generally, the largest continuous source of air pollution in the world is from human activities. Sometimes air pollution is visible and we can see it in the air surrounding our cities. Soot from fires and other sources of combustion creates visible air pollution.

In the Maritimes we have two strikes against us. First, we have among the heaviest reliance on fossil fuels in the world for our heat and energy generation. The second is that since weather flows from west to east, and virtually all of North America is west of us, including the very industrialized eastern US and Canada, we also get their effluent in addition to producing our own. It's almost an even split. Half of our pollution is home-produced and half comes from the continental heartland.

Sometimes air pollution is invisible and gaseous, but it is still there and changes the nature of the air we breathe. Ground-level ozone is like that. It's virtually invisible and odourless, but is a very harmful gas when found at ground level and is very dangerous to breathe. It is caused by things like the exhaust of automobiles interacting with sunlight.

Smog is, quite literally, the air we see in our cities. It's a combination of two words, smoke and fog. Smog is dirty air created from the exhaust of cars and other internal combustion engines, fires for cooking and warmth, and the generation of power from coal-fired and oil-fired power plants.

Since the early Industrial Revolution when most industrial activity was powered by coal, London has been famous for its lethal combination of smoke and fog. Because of a shortage of indigenous oil until the 1960s the use of coal for heat and industry in the UK continued into modern times.

The smoke-laden fog that shrouded London from Friday, December 5 to Tuesday, December 9, 1952, brought premature death to thousands and inconvenience to millions. An estimated 4,000 people died and cattle at Smithfield were asphyxiated. Road, rail and air transport were almost brought to a standstill and a performance at the Sadler's Wells Theatre had to be suspended when fog in the auditorium made conditions intolerable for the audience and performers.

The death toll was not disputed by medical and other authorities, but exactly how many people perished as a direct result of the fog will never be known. Many who died already suffered from chronic respiratory or cardiovascular complaints. Without the fog, they might not have died when they did. The total number of deaths in Greater London in the week ending December 6, 1952, was 2,062, which was close to normal for the time of year. The following week, the number was 4,703. The death rate peaked at 900 per day on the 8th and 9th and remained above average until just before Christmas. Mortality from bronchitis and pneumonia increased more than sevenfold as a result of the fog.

The very young, very old and sick suffer the most during bouts of smog. And no city is without smog problems. Los Angeles has probably the worst smog in the United States, while Mexico City and Beijing set the standards for some of the worst air in the world. Both are among the ten most populous cities in the world, with Mexico City having just over half as many people as the entire country of Canada. As of January 1, 2008, Canada's population was just under 33 million and Mexico City's population was estimated to be 18 million.

In general, because smog is usually quite localized, no area of the Maritimes has yet had a significant smog problem on the scale of what has been happening to Ontario. During the summer months an inversion (a stable configuration of cooler air topped by warmer air aloft) can often trap smog for a few days at a time and create those hazy, stifling days where breathing is difficult. But this only happens in the Maritimes once or twice a year. Though the number of smog days in Halifax and Saint John have risen slightly, the flow of weather from west to east and the effects of the ocean ensure that they don't last more than a few days. In Toronto the contrast in the past two decades has been startling. Toronto rarely had smog alerts before the 1970s. Now they occur on average at least once a week during the height of the summer, where people are requested to refrain from using automobiles and running air conditioners.

According to Environment Canada, the concern about smog in the Maritimes is rising because air pollutants can be transported 800 kilometres downwind in a single day from places like Quebec, Ontario and the eastern United States. Recent medical studies have identified an increase in hospital admissions with deteriorating air quality. Air pollution and ground-level ozone levels in the Maritimes are worst in May, June, July and August when the summer sunshine interacts with atmospheric oxides to produce ozone.

Global warming gases, or greenhouse gases, are gases that contribute to the warming of the planet and, unlike air pollution and smog, are not visible. The main GWGs are carbon dioxide, water vapour, methane and some of the oxide gases. They are a normal part of the atmosphere and play a vital role in keeping it at a comfortable temperature for life on Earth. If the Earth did not have GWGs it would freeze solid. On the other hand, if greenhouse gas levels were too high, the Earth's temperature would increase to the point that it would be too hot for life. And this is the problem with human-induced greenhouse gases. In addition to air pollution, we also make greenhouse gases through our industry.

The Greenhouse Effect, the Goldilocks Effect and Greenhouse Gases

The greenhouse effect gets its name from the similarity between how glass in a greenhouse works to how some gases in the atmosphere behave. The light of the sun has a great deal of energy and, for the most part, the atmosphere, like glass, is transparent to the light from the sun. The light strikes the surface of the Earth and is absorbed. The energy that is absorbed is then re-emitted from the surface as heat, infrared radiation. This energy is of a different wavelength than the original light that shines in from the sun. Now this is the interesting part. There are some gases which are almost opaque to heat and trap it. This is the same as glass. Light gets in, but the heat is trapped. These gases are called the greenhouse gases.

Just like pollution, not all greenhouse gases are created equal when it comes to their ability to trap heat. There are a number of gases that are very good at trapping heat in the atmosphere. The four main greenhouse gases are carbon dioxide, methane, water vapour and nitrous oxide. Of these, water vapour accounts for the greatest greenhouse effect with between 35 to 70 percent of the total effect, carbon dioxide at 10 to 25 percent, methane at 5 to 10 percent and nitrous oxide at 3 to 5 percent. Other greenhouse gases include, but are not limited to, ozone, sulfur hexafluoride, hydrofluorocarbons, perfluorocarbons and chloro-fluorocarbons. The main gases of the Earth's atmosphere, nitrogen (78 percent of the total) and oxygen (21 percent), are not greenhouse gases because they neither absorb nor emit infra-red or heat radiation. And even though the four main green-house gases make up less than 1 percent of the total mass of the Earth's atmosphere, they account for almost all its greenhouse effect.

When life first began on Earth, the sun was dimmer and the atmosphere was over 90 percent CO_2. Early anaerobic life consumed the carbon dioxide with a vengeance through a photosynthetic process that emitted O_2, oxygen. As the O_2 levels increased and the CO_2 level fell, the greenhouse effect was diminished on Earth as the sun warmed. This allowed the Earth to maintain a stable temperature, without heating up too much as the sun grew warmer. It was an amazing process and kept the Earth from boiling away its oceans, as would have happened if anaerobes had not consumed the CO_2 and created O_2.

For the past three to four billion years the temperature of the Earth has been carefully regulated by an amazing variety of feedback loops, which James Lovelock called the Gaia Hypothesis.

Earth is the only planet that has been able to have a stable temperature and environment for life and it has done so for over three and a half billion years. In that time the sun's brightness has increased 25 percent. Even though the sun has become substantially brighter and its energy output has increased over the billions of years that life has existed on Earth, the temperature of the environment has remained consistent.

Comparing Earth to the other planets of the solar system closest to us we find Venus too hot for life, Mars too cold, but Earth is just right. This is sometimes termed the Goldilocks Effect. This expression comes from the children's fairy tale *Goldilocks and the Three Bears*. Goldilocks finds the bears' three bowls of porridge, and one was too hot, one was too cold and the last just right.

Without the warming effect of the greenhouse gases Earth's average temperature would be much cooler and severe in its fluctuations. They act as a thermal blanket, keeping the Earth and its living ecosystem within certain safe bounds.

Because of the ocean, the Maritimes are very vulnerable to changes in the weather brought about by water vapour. Even though water vapour is a serious greenhouse gas – and as the average global temperature climbs, more is produced because of evaporation – there's another factor which works to diminish this effect. Clouds have a blocking effect. They are made up of tiny water droplets and not water vapour. They are highly reflective and keep the sun's rays from reaching the surface.

What this means is that if more water vapour is produced, it's probable that more clouds will also be produced. Whether this means that cloud production will mitigate the increased greenhouse effect of the water vapour is still not certain. Cloud physicists feel it is likely the increased water vapour will win out. They point to Venus, our planetary neighbour, which has evaporated its oceans and is entirely shrouded by brilliant white clouds, yet has the highest surface temperature of any planet in the solar system.

Even though the four main greenhouse gases are similar to one another because each warms the Earth, they are also vastly different from each other. Water vapour, the gas responsible for the greatest greenhouse effect, is not uniformly spread throughout the atmosphere. Over the liquid oceans, where it is expected, its effect is greatest. In terms of weather and climate, water vapour is the most important of all the gases, even though its total mass in the atmosphere is tiny, less than one-half of 1 percent. Without water and its ability to store energy and give off energy as it changes state, from liquid to gas and solid within the normal temperatures of the Earth, there would be a remarkably different atmosphere, and climate as we know it would not exist. In short, water is a most amazing substance and its importance to life on Earth cannot in any way be overstated.

Over the great inland deserts, where there is little water vapour and the prevailing winds come from land-based regions, the amount of water vapour is almost zero in the atmosphere. These areas are noted for having great fluctuations in temperature and for their consistently dry weather patterns. As long as the average temperature of Earth stays within certain bounds the total water vapour content of the atmosphere remains the same.

Methane and ozone in the atmosphere, though substantial contributors to the greenhouse effect, are quite volatile and react with their surroundings much more than CO_2, so they have to be constantly replenished by natural and, recently, human processes in order for their levels to stay constant. In the case of human activities, if people cut down their production of methane and ozone in industry and agriculture, the levels will settle quite rapidly back to natural levels to which the ecosystem has adjusted.

The case of carbon dioxide (CO_2) is where we come into serious concerns in its global warming interactions and human development. CO_2 is a very stable and long-lived molecule and is chemically unreactive, unlike methane, which burns and bonds quite readily with other elements and compounds. Methane reacts strongly with sunlight and other substances, especially free oxygen (O_2). CO_2 is already in a very tight bond with oxygen, a very voracious element, and is the end result of any combustive process.

The chemically inert CO_2 is then absorbed by the ecosystem and oceans. Plants, bacteria and other anaerobic single-celled organisms consume and extract CO_2 from the atmosphere and then use light from the sun in a process called photosynthesis, which breaks apart the strong carbon-oxygen bond to create free carbon and free oxygen. The carbon is used as a body building element because it can combine in a huge number of ways with just about any element, while the oxygen is discarded as a waste product.

Primordial Earth: How it all Began

Like Venus and Mars, Earth is one of a group of inner solar system planets small enough that hydrogen and helium do not form the main constituents of their atmospheres.

Hydrogen is by far the most abundant element in the universe, forming almost three-quarters of its visible mass. Helium, the second lightest element, forms just under a quarter with all the rest of the elements of the periodic table at just about 1 percent.

Helium is too light for any of the terrestrial planets to hold gravitationally. Virtually all of the helium in the Earth's atmosphere comes from the radioactive processes in the crust that release alpha particles, which are just a helium nucleus of two protons and two neutrons. The alpha particle, once emitted, attracts two electrons to make up the helium atom. However, helium is notoriously inert and does not bond with anything and remains a free atom in gaseous form. It, too, rapidly escapes from the Earth's relatively feeble gravitational bonds.

What started out as a uniform and universal reflection of the element distribution rapidly became reorganized. The much larger Jovian planets, the Latin name for Jupiter (Saturn, Uranus and Neptune are the others), had masses large enough to retain their original atmospheres of hydrogen, helium and methane around their rocky/metallic cores, while the smaller terrestrial planets evolved. They lost their lighter elements and retained the heavier ones.

Though volcanic outgassing continued because internal radioactivity, tidal forces, comets and meteors brought other rare elements and compounds to the planets, within the first half billion years the makeup of the planets and their atmospheres was basically complete and divided between the two groups, the massive gas giants and the smaller terrestrial planets.

It appears that Earth alone carried the evolution of its atmosphere to the next level. On Earth, life evolved. It remains to be seen whether life evolved anywhere else.

The next step is one that continues to amaze me.

If Earth had retained its original atmospheric makeup after the loss of the lighter hydrogen and helium, the remaining dominant gas, CO_2, would have and did compose about 95 percent of the total atmospheric content. This is astounding since both Venus and Mars reflect this percentage today, and it jives well with the theories of the progress and evolution of their atmospheres and the solar system. Three and a half billion years ago three of the four terrestrial planets, the lone exception being Mercury, were all places where the temperature was just right for liquid, solid and gaseous water to exist. The combination of carbon dioxide and water vapour created a greenhouse effect in the proper range for this to happen.

Mercury failed to retain its atmosphere because it was even smaller than Mars and so close to the sun. The huge solar wind pressure pretty much stripped it of any atmosphere it originally had. Today it has effectively no atmosphere and is just a rock with huge temperature fluctuations, orbiting some 56 million kilometres from the sun, three times closer than the earth, receiving ten times the radiation that we do.

As the nuclear processes within the sun evolved, the sun began to speed up its reactions and it became brighter, by some

25 percent. If life ever existed on Venus it soon died because the oceans of Venus evaporated and the entire atmosphere heated to hundreds of degrees hotter than the Earth's.

Within a short period of time Mars too lost its potential to support life, because it was too small to hold on to its atmosphere and too far away from the sun.

But on the Earth life had evolved. It was a photosynthetic life that consumed CO_2 and used the sun's energy to separate the tightly bound oxygen and carbon. The carbon was metabolized and the oxygen was a waste and expelled into the atmosphere. There was so much carbon dioxide to consume in the atmosphere that life literally exploded in the warm oceans. From the fossil evidence it appears the ocean surface was completely covered by mats of these anaerobic microscopic creatures. There were trillions upon trillions of these creatures consuming CO_2, converting it in the warm sunshine to oxygen and carbon, eating the carbon, making it part of the food chain and expelling the oxygen. Fossils of these creatures called stromatolites have been found on Ellesmere Island and their living anaerobic descendants still flourish in hypersaline tropical pools like Shark's Bay, Australia.

A billion years ago life in the Maritimes consisted of a variety of primeval life: stromatolites, symbiotic, tiny creatures living in vast colonies of mats floating in all the oceans, mircroscopic prokaryotes (single-celled creatures like bacteria, without nuclei), and eukaryotes (single-celled creatures whose cells have nuclei). There were no animals or plants or any of the creatures that we recognize today. The oxygen of the atmosphere was just beginning to reach today's levels.

The net result was that, slowly, over a couple of billion years, the CO_2 levels fell and oxygen at first combined with just about anything that it could because of its voracious valence and propensity for creating compounds. But at some point all the available bonding was complete, as oxygen saturated the crustal rocks. Oxygen then began to accumulate in the atmosphere.

The First Mass Extinction: Oxygen Toxicity

It was a classic case of too much of a good thing. The oxygen the anaerobes excreted was a waste and a highly toxic one. At first the oxygen accumulation was too low to really affect the anaerobes. It was absorbed by the environment and because of its volatility was soon bonded into less harmful, inert compounds.

But as oxygen levels rose, it began to have a deleterious effect. It was very destructive to DNA and complex proteins of life. Where oxygen accumulated, anaerobes died off.

In the atmosphere, as oxygen levels began to rise, it also dissolved in the ocean water and accumulated. The massive, almost uncountable, numbers of anaerobes produced oxygen prodigiously. As they did so, there was a corresponding drop in CO_2 levels. Carbon was being taken from the atmosphere, deposited into the ecosystem and free oxygen was being released.

Oxygen is not a greenhouse gas. As the sun became brighter, the corresponding drop in CO_2 and its replacement with O_2 meant the temperature of the Earth did not rise.

Oxygen levels in the atmosphere began to rise. It had saturated the crust with oxides and was now entering the atmosphere. This was perhaps the first pollution in the world's history. And the anaerobes were beginning to feel its effects.

The drop in CO_2 had catastrophic effects on the Earth. The amount of CO_2 dropped so far that there is evidence anaerobic life nearly undid their almost perfect environment. The geological remains from about 800 million years ago strongly indicate that Earth was beset by the most massive ice age in its 4.65 billion-year history. It seems the entire Earth froze. Even the tropical oceans were covered in ice. It was a time that paleontologists call

Snowball Earth. It lasted 100 to 200 million years and its impact on life on the Earth, on the anaerobic creatures, was catastrophic. Life on Earth almost came to an end.

The carbon dioxide levels fell so far that the greenhouse effect was not enough to keep the average temperature of the Earth warm enough to prevent the water from freezing. Once the water froze, so did the ecosystem in which the anaerobes lived. In addition to losing their CO_2 greenhouse gas because of their voracious carbon appetites, once the oceans froze over they also lost water vapour in the atmosphere. It was a double greenhouse gas whammy. The temperature plummeted and it seemed as though Earth would be a frozen lifeless planet as the anaerobes died out.

But the Earth's plate tectonic processes rescued the climate. As the plates shifted they opened fissures in the crust, volcanoes erupted and replenished the CO_2 enough so that after a few thousand years or so, the Earth warmed sufficiently for the oceans to melt and the ice to retreat.

By this time the anaerobes had almost died out and existed in just a tiny part of the Earth. Most of the CO_2 had been consumed; what was now in the atmosphere was but a fraction of the amount it had previously been. The levels of the toxic gas oxygen were so high that anaerobes could not reclaim the oceans and take advantage of the opening of the oceans after the big freeze. But life hung on in the strangest places. In the thermal vents deep in the oceans, on the boundaries of the crustal plates that were driven by magma moving deep within the Earth's mantle, there was enough heat and warmth for life to survive. The new life that evolved here was able to take advantage of the new atmosphere, one where oxygen, O_2, was one of the dominant gases.

In the space of just a few million years, life on Earth flowered in a way never before or since seen. The new creatures in the thermal vents had evolved enough in their hostile environment to not only be able to tolerate oxygen, but to thrive on it. They were able to use oxygen as part of their metabolism, giving them a stupendous advantage. Oxygen became a new supermetabolic fuel. By harnessing oxygen's voracious appetite to bond with other elements into the metabolic process, these new aerobic, oxygen-consuming creatures were able to outdo the ancient slower anaerobes in the exploitation of the new oxygen-dominated ecosystem. Life transformed and expanded. Plants, animals, fungi, bacteria, and a host of other phyla sprang into being. In a geologic heartbeat life had adapted to the killer gas oxygen, co-opted it as a major constituent of the metabolic process and never looked back. By half a billion years ago, the dominant life on Earth had spread into all the ocean niches and was just beginning to embark on the great assault on land.

Almost all the fossils found in the Maritimes come from the Phanerozoic era, the past 545 million years. All the coal deposits, bones and tracks date from relatively recent times, after the great flowering of life in the Pre-cambrian era, after Snowball Earth.

Oxygen became the gas on which life thrived; new species developed and took the evolutionary track into places and complexities never before seen.

Through it all, the expanding diversity exploited every niche conceivable, first the oceans, then the land and air. Plants, bacteria and archaic anaerobes continued to supply oxygen into the atmosphere on which virtually all life became dependent, because without replenishment it would disappear in a matter of hundreds of years.

Earth became unique and self-sustaining, life intricately interwoven with the oceans, land and atmosphere in a fabulous feedback loop. It is called the ecosphere, a thin band a few tens of kilometres thick completely surrounding the Earth, where all life that we know about existed and exists. In the past 500 million years we have had first the ocean crustaceans, like trilobites, dominate life, then in succession, fishes, amphibians, reptiles and now mammals, flowering plants and insects.

The Milankovitch Cycles

The Earth, its orbit around the sun and the tilt that the Earth has in relation to the plane of its orbit are not fixed and permanent. Milutin Milankovitch (1879-1958), a Serbian mathematician and engineer, came up with the theory (The Milankovitch Theory) that the eccentricity of the Earth's orbit, the varying of the tilt of the Earth's rotational axis, and the variations in the precession of the equinoxes and solstices are responsible for the sequence of ice ages during the Pleistocene era.

Because of the Milankovitch Cycles the Maritimes have changed regularly and often during the past three million years of the Pleistocene era. Glaciers advanced and retreated, alternately covering and exposing the Maritimes. Ocean levels have risen and fallen by 120 metres, causing the Maritimes to shrink and grow in a converse relation to the ocean levels. For example, 21,000 years ago Sable Island was larger than Cape Breton Island is today when the ocean was more than 100 metres lower. Both Bedford Basin and the Bras d'Or lakes, now saltwater bodies, were once freshwater lakes far above sea level.

The Earth's orbit around the sun is anything but simple. It's not a perfect circle but an ellipse, which means at some times in its orbit it is closer to the sun than at others. But the shape of the ellipse also changes. It is sometimes more circular than at other times and its shape varies according to a number of complex cycles that vary over tens of thousands of years. Not only does the ellipse change, but the tilt of the Earth also changes with respect to the plane of the orbit. Finally, the ellipse precesses – that is, the closest point to the sun changes over time.

It appears, because of the Milankovitch Cycles and the current placement of the continents, that we are in the middle of an ice age and if there were no human influences to consider, the ice would again advance. All of Canada, the northern half of the United States and much of Europe would again be under ice kilometres thick.

The placement of Antarctica over the South Pole, the massive Himalayan plateau created by India smashing into central Asia, the creation of an isthmus linking North and South America, and the Milankovitch Cycles all conspired at the same time to thrust the Earth's climate into the cycle of retreating and advancing ice sheets, the latest ice age.

The cooling of the Earth that led to the ice ages began to happen 40 million years ago as Antarctica drifted south to cover the South Pole. Up until this time the Earth had no permanent ice caps and the climate was universally mild. Even the far north and far south didn't have permanent snow and ice. Plate tectonics created the rift that separated Africa from South America and North America from Europe. The Atlantic Ocean was beginning to appear and 40 million years ago was a fraction of its size today. This influenced the ocean circulation patterns, which influenced how the heat from the equator, the warmest part of the Earth, was distributed to the rest of the world. The deep ocean began to cool and currents began to change.

In the past three million years the final pieces listed above were put into place and the massive ice ages began.

When the ice advance begins again in the northern hemisphere (the question is when, not if), the Maritimes will see a rapid onset of ice sheets that will cover the same areas that have recently seen the ice retreat. The ocean levels will plummet and the land area will grow by 20 percent.

2

What is Changing

The Temperature Profile

There is absolutely no dispute that the planet is getting warmer. As we get better at measuring the warmth of the planet we reaffirm what has been the general consensus among atmospheric scientists. The graph on page 50 illustrates exactly what has been measured. Since 1940 the warmth of our planet has increased more than half a degree Celsius.

There are places, such as the Caribbean and parts of western Africa, where the mean temperature has stayed the same. A few places have even cooled. The western Antarctic and southeastern Atlantic coast of the United States are definitely cooler. But on the whole, the warmer temperatures dominate. The really troubling part is that the most dramatic warming of the decade is happening in the Arctic of North America, Europe and Asia. And here is why.

If we examine the temperature profile carefully, we see that the temperature increases seem to be small. On the average, it appears to be less than a two-degree Celsius increase. It doesn't

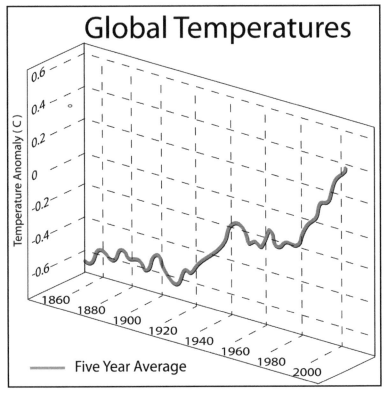

Average global temperature increases over the past 150 years.

seem to be much but it is enough to change the climate dramatically. It is especially problematic in areas that receive seasonal variances involving snow.

The ability of a substance to absorb or reflect light is called albedo. Soot has a very low albedo because it is black and almost all the light that falls on it is absorbed and very little reflected back. Snow has a high albedo – that is, it is almost perfectly white and reflects almost all the sunlight than falls on it without absorbing the energy or heat. Because of this it stays cold and preserves itself. But if it warms and melts, the albedo of snow changes and it then absorbs far more light and heat.

NOAA, the National Oceanographic and Atmospheric Administration of the United States, declared the winter of 2006-07 the warmest in recorded history globally. In the Maritimes it was a warmer than average winter, which had incredibly warm temperatures till mid-January. Once the cold weather began, it only lasted six or seven weeks before the spring weather resurged. In addition, precipitation amounts remained below normal.

During the winter, a record number of wells had far below normal water table levels and some went dry, a very unusual occurrence. Lakes all across the region were lower, water tables lower and river flows reduced. If this trend to mild weather and below normal precipitation continues in the Maritimes, there will be serious changes to water levels in lakes, rivers and groundwater tables.

Frozen water, whether ice and snow or solid water, can absorb heat without changing to a liquid at 0°C. To melt, ice and snow must absorb massive amounts of heat/energy. This is called a change of state. And this works in reverse. Once you have put the energy/heat into the ice and it melts, in order to freeze the water back into ice you must get rid of that heat.

Even though it requires an enormous amount of energy to convert ice into heat, most of the glaciers covering the Maritimes, some half million cubic kilometres of ice, melted in just 5,000 years, along with the rest of the Wisconsin ice sheet. The energy needed to melt all the glaciers would be equivalent to raising the global air temperature by more than 20 degrees Celsius all around the world.

Water moderates weather. Fluctuations in temperature are not nearly as big in wet climates as they are in drier areas of the world. The change of state from liquid to solid and back again has so much latent heat that it prevents large temperature changes. You wind up getting a lot of precipitation, but your temperature profile in the winter months is not as cold, nor is the summer as hot, as it is in drier climates.

Ice also moderates and controls temperature. It takes energy to melt ice. To melt the global ice caps great amounts of energy have to be put into the ecosystem. The heat put into the ice is stored in the melted ice water.

In places where there is permanent ice twelve months of the year we have noticed not only increases in temperature, but also melting, indicating that there are great changes coming.

The largest buffer to climate change in the northern hemisphere is the Arctic ice. Once the ice melts, the water will increase its temperature even faster because it absorbs so much more of the light and heat that falls on it.

Ocean Levels

Current measurements of the Arctic ice cap show it has decreased in total mass by about 30 percent over the past three decades. Given that the process is now accelerating, estimates are we will lose the remaining 70 percent in about 30 years.

Why have we not noticed it before? If all this ice has melted why haven't we seen a dramatic rise in ocean levels? The answer is the ice in the Arctic Ocean floats in the water, in the same way that ice in a glass floats in the water. In both cases as the ice melts, the water level stays the same because the ice is already in the glass or the ocean.

However, the ice and snow on land in the form of ice caps and glaciers is a very different story. Ice on land that melts is water added to the ocean and you set the stage for a rise in ocean levels.

With the climate changing the rise in ocean levels has become an issue. More than a third of the total human population live within 100 kilometres of the ocean and 80 percent live within 100 kilometres of a major body of water, so something like a change in ocean levels would be of serious concern.

To put things into perspective, the world's ocean levels have been fluctuating for their entire existence and have at some time been much higher and at other times much lower than they are today. For instance, at the height of the last glacial advance, 23,000 years ago, when enormous amounts of the world's water were tied up in the vast glaciers that covered Europe and North America, the ocean levels were 130 to 140 metres lower than they are currently. At first the sea level rise was prodigious. Rates were as much as three metres a century in the first few thousand years.

Twenty-three thousands years ago, because they were covered by a vast weight of ice, much of the Maritimes were under sea level, even though the ocean level was much lower than it is today. As the levels rose when the ice sheets melted, the crustal plate under the ice rebounded even more quickly than the sea levels. Today the rise is still continuing, though at a very slow rate. Many beaches in the Maritimes which were at sea level 12,000 years ago are now well above sea level. The most spectacular example is Cape Chignecto, which is almost 40 metres above the current sea levels.

The current rate of the Greenland melt is adding about two millimetres of water a year to the ocean levels, which is about ten times the amount it was adding a decade ago. It doesn't seem like much, but over the years its inexorable march adds up.

Another millimetre of water level is being added because of thermal expansion. As the ocean's average temperature rises, the water expands, taking up more space. This makes warm water slightly deeper than cold water.

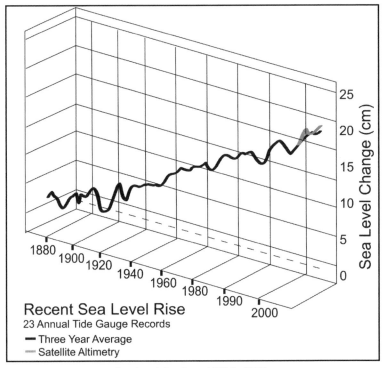

Recent Sea Level Rise
23 Annual Tide Gauge Records
— Three Year Average
— Satellite Altimetry

Sea level rise from 1880 to 2000.

One hundred years ago the ocean levels were rising at a much slower rate than they are today and were 20 centimetres lower. The rate began to increase about 1910 and has remained at a consistent rate until the past decade. The rate over the past five years has increased dramatically and the rate of the increase is increasing. Most of the increase in the ocean levels is because the melt of the Greenland ice cap has accelerated dramatically, by an unbelievable factor of ten.

In addition to the ice cap melt contributing to rising ocean levels, water expands as it warms. In other words, if you had a column of water 10,000 metres deep it would be 10,002 metres if you raised the temperature six degrees. The average depth of the world's oceans is 3,700 metres and if the ocean's temperature increased six degrees, it would be 74 centimetres deeper.

This is a very significant amount. Because research into the changes in the ocean's temperature profile is in its relative infancy, it is, at this stage, hard to definitely quantify how quickly the oceans are warming. We do know the transfer of heat in the oceans is very slow and once warming occurs it can take hundreds and even thousands of years to completely distribute itself throughout the water column. The rate of increase from thermal expansion from 1993 to 2003 was determined to be three millimetres a year and accelerating. Because water takes such a long time to transfer heat, the expansion will continue for a long time even if the effects of climate change were mitigated. Rising ocean levels are a fact of life and are going to be with us for some time.

Generally, conservative estimates expect the ocean levels to rise anywhere from 20 to 80 centimetres over the next 50 years, if the current melt levels do not accelerate beyond projections and if thermal expansion rates remain low. But new studies show these numbers may be low and some models indicate that between thermal expansion and the ice melt, we could have increases as high as 150 to 300 centimetres. And it does appear that the melt is increasing and even the Antarctic is contributing to the rising levels. New information and studies becoming available are indicating that the Intergovernmental Panel on Climate and Change (IPCC) projections may be low.

Sixteen thousand years ago the sea level off Halifax was some 40 metres lower than it is today. By 8,000 years rebound had occurred and Halifax was 65 metres above sea level, even though the global oceans had risen more than 80 metres. Bedford Basin in Halifax was an inland lake only 9,000 years ago. Prince Edward Island remained a part of the mainland until about 8,000 years ago and now PEI has erosion of half a metre per year.

It is important to understand that ocean levels in the past 130,000 years have risen and fallen spectacularly. At the height of the last interglacial, sea levels were five to six metres higher than they are today. The evidence suggests that during every interglacial much or even all of the Greenland ice sheet melts.

When the volume of the Greenland ice sheet is taken into account and distributed throughout the world's oceans we see that this, in fact, is the five or six metres that we are missing. Researchers measuring the age of the Greenland ice find it is only about 110,000 years old. In contrast, places in Antarctica are over 500,000 years old, with the cores telling us of shifting milder climates at regular 100,000-year cycles.

As the Earth warms, the melt will accelerate and the Earth's shoreline will change dramatically. A change in sea level of even half a metre will devastate many shorelines. And in the Maritimes we can expect many changes.

Assuming that all the ice of Greenland melts, as it has for every interglacial of the past three million years, that would create a new sea level five to six metres higher than it is today. Assuming a horizontal reach of about 100 to one over the vertical, this would mean that a rise of five metres would on average create erosion of half a kilometre. This means the coastline of the Maritimes would be dramatically altered, especially shores that are sandy and have low gradients.

Currently the sea level rise of two millimetres per year is creating an erosion of half a metre on PEI's sandy Gulf of St. Lawrence shores, a factor of 250. Extrapolating the next century's worth of ocean rise at one metre would bring a devastating 250 metres of erosion, enough to put most of downtown Charlottetown in a swampy, brackish bog.

Until 2000 few studies had taken into account the Antarctic's effect on the rise and fall of the ocean levels because it has, by and large, remained fast and frozen through all the cycles of the advance and retreats of the northern ice fields in the past two to three million years. New information tells us that this time around, given that greenhouse gas levels are rising to unprecedented levels, we may have to factor in this continent's huge store of ice. The fracturing of the Larsen B shelf, in the western Antarctic, has almost definitely happened because of the climate warming. Studies by Chris Rapley of the British Antarctic Survey in 2005 indicate the melt has been underestimated and that in fact the Antarctic melt has accelerated. If this happens, then the estimates of sea level increase would be low by a very large factor. Should it all melt, sea levels would rise 120 metres higher than they are today, levels not seen in 40 million years.

The last time the Earth was without permanent ice we have to go back 40 million years to the Eocene Epoch, a time when the Earth was a far, far warmer place and looked much different than it does today. The land area was smaller, the ocean area larger and there were no permanent ice sheets over the poles. But as the Antarctic continent drifted over the South Pole permanent ice began to form. It took almost ten million years for the ice sheet to completely envelop the Antarctic, but once it happened and the continent remained over the South Pole, its ice sheet became a permanent fixture. Ocean levels dropped and more and more water was contained in the ice.

Then about three million years ago the fastest moving continent in the Earth's history slammed into Asia. India moving north and pushing into the belly of Asia created the greatest mountain range and the highest plateau on Earth, the Himalayas. These mountains and their attendant plateau are so dominant and large that they affect the airflow pattern of the Earth and allow very cold air to dominate much of the northern hemisphere for much of the winter season. This, coupled with the Milankovitch Cycles, allowed the current ice age cycle to begin in earnest.

> Plate tectonics continue to widen the gap between the Maritimes and Europe. The island of Iceland, which straddles the mid-oceanic rift, is an example of the volcanism that exists on the boundaries between the various crustal plates. The expansion of the Atlantic Ocean is about four centimetres per year, though the rate has varied over the millions of years since the original rifting occurred. In about 50 million years the gap between the Maritimes and Europe will approach its maximum, creating the world's largest ocean, some 10,000 kilometres across.

Now that the pattern is set there appears to be no end to the current ice age cycle until the continents are redistributed in such a way that the warmth of the equator can find its way to the poles more efficiently.

The Milankovitch Cycles will cause the ice advance to come and go, but will not permanently stop the advances of continental glaciers. This cycle has been going on for almost three million years. But now that people have added so much CO_2 to the atmosphere we have to consider what this will do. Is it possible, now that the CO_2 levels have reached higher levels than at any other interglacial, that we will kick the climate out of the ice ages permanently?

That is the question climatologists are trying desperately to answer. Most of the models show that once the carbon dioxide levels are 50 percent higher than they have been in past interglacials, a tipping point is reached. The levels today are around 400 parts per million and already higher than the highest observed levels for any interglacial.

In fact, when we look for past examples of CO_2 levels higher than they are today, we have to track back a quarter of a billion years ago, to the Permian Extinction, the greatest crisis ever to affect life on Earth. What happened? The climate just got too hot. A runaway greenhouse effect was created, life almost died out completely and it took millions of years for the climate to settle back to normal.

It appears that at a certain point, the carbon dioxide concentration gets so high that the oceans become too warm, creating additional water vapour and releasing it into the atmosphere. Water vapour is an even better greenhouse gas than CO_2 and heats up the atmosphere even more in a positive feedback loop.

It all centres around the most important and critical greenhouse gas, carbon dioxide.

Carbon Dioxide

Carbon dioxide is the most important greenhouse gas in the atmosphere from a number of standpoints and as such, its levels are the most intensely scrutinized of all the GHGs. The past record tells us when the CO_2 levels are high, so is the temperature and when the levels are low, so also is the average global temperature.

We can get a snapshot of air by examining the ice from very old glaciers on Greenland and Antarctica. When snow falls and accumulates, tiny bubbles of air become trapped inside the snow. When the snow is compressed into ice, the air is locked within the ice and becomes a permanent time capsule of what the air was like at the time it was originally trapped.

The most detailed research comes from core samples in the glaciers in Greenland. As Greenland is more accessible than Antarctica more research has been done on its ice cap. It is also the ice field that will have the most direct effect on Europe and North America when it melts.

But the Greenland ice sheet vanishes every 130,000 years or so and then reforms when the climate again becomes cold and the ice again advances. So no ice core older than 100,000 years or one cycle can be obtained from Greenland. What may have happened in previous advances is left to other research methods or from the cores of Antarctic ice.

One method is to examine old beaches from previous sea level maximums. Many ancient beaches are found in the

Maritimes and they all seem to indicate that the difference in the water levels currently and in the past match well with the amount of water contained from the melted ice. Horton Bluff is an example of an ancient beach in Avonport, Nova Scotia. This beach dates from Devonian times when the Earth was warmer than it is today and likely had very little permanent ice. In other places like St. Mary's Bay, on Nova Scotia's Bay of Fundy shore, we have many raised beaches, evidence of higher water levels, coastal rebound and tilting following the glacial withdrawal. We can also see submerged forests and coastal submergence of cliffs and beaches when water levels were lower.

Antarctic ice has been around much longer than Greenland ice and Antarctica itself has been close to the South Pole for almost 40 million years. Ice cores from Antarctica corroborate the Greenland cores for the past 100,000 or so years. Researchers have been able to extract cores in Antarctica with ice more than half a million years old or four glacial advances. They have found that the carbon dioxide levels from the cores rise and fall in close cadence with global temperatures. Each and every CO_2 peak is matched with the warmest global temperatures and the CO_2 minimums happen during the coldest periods.

Ice Thickness and Extent During the Last Glacial Advance

The last time the Earth was this warm was during the last interglacial or warming, roughly 130,000 years ago. If you had been around then the world would not have looked much different than it does today, though some of the animals might have given you a bit of a surprise.

This was a time of mammoths, mastodons, saber-toothed cats, glyptodons, ground sloths, and short-faced bears, which are all now extinct. The forest regions, grasslands, deserts and ocean habitats would have been filled with recognizable flora and fauna, a virtual Eden of life.

The last interglacial lasted about 20,000 years. At its warmest nearly all of Greenland would have been almost totally free of permanent ice and its melted ice would have made sea levels about six or seven metres higher than they are today.

During the last interglacial Nova Scotia was almost an island. What we now call the mainland was almost separated from New Brunswick with ocean water creating a brackish swamp across the lowland running from Prince Edward Island to the Bay of Fundy. PEI was much reduced and cut into three smaller islands. Ocean water flooded much of the St. John River and many of what are now coastal communities of all three provinces would have been in serious difficulty.

This high sea level would not have lasted long because interglacials are relatively short compared to ice advances. In as little as 10,000 years, the warming was over and snowfall amounts increased, global climate dropped by three to five degrees Celsius and the ice began its inexorable march southwards. The ocean levels would have dropped precipitously as the ice levels on the continents rose. The Earth's coasts would move tens and even hundreds of kilometres seaward as the ocean levels dropped.

For almost 100,000 years the ice maintained its grip on the world's climate. The entire Atlantic Canada coast was buried under three to four kilometres of permanent ice. All of Atlantic Canada would have resembled what we see in modern-day Antarctica – vast white, glistening plateaus of ice calving giant icebergs into the surrounding ocean.

Because of the continental positions, Milankovitch Cycles, atmospheric composition and ocean currents we became locked in the cycle of glacial advance and retreat. Like some giant climate switch clicking back and forth we cycled from warm to cold every 100,000 years or so and would likely continue to do so for

Most rocks in the Maritimes are younger than one billion years of age. Areas in Cape Breton, Antigonish and southern New Brunswick are among the oldest in the Maritimes and date to the second youngest supercontinent, Rodinia. This makes the Maritime region very young compared to the Canadian Shield and the Laurentians, which are among the oldest rocks on Earth, close to four billion years.

many millions of years, if it wasn't for the fact that we are now changing the greenhouse gases rules.

The Global Ocean Conveyor

The oceans and their relationship to the climate have been a bit of a mystery over the years because we spend so little time on and in them. Though we collect information about the oceans, it is often just surface information and what goes on below the oceans' surface had remained, for the most part, unknown.

In the past few decades, satellites, computers and very sophisticated sensors have begun to pull back the information veil of the oceans and what we are finding is nothing short of amazing.

There is a band of moving water, a river if you like, that traverses the entire globe and it transports more energy from the equator to the poles than the entire atmosphere does. It's called the Global Ocean Conveyor. What creates and drives the Ocean Conveyor is the difference in density of ocean water from different parts of the world. The difference in density is in part due to the difference in temperature of the water and in part due to salinity. Both the differences in salinity and temperature cause changes in density in the water, which in turn cause it to rise or sink. And this difference in density is what ultimately causes the water to move from one part of the globe to another.

The Gulf Stream is a small part of the Ocean Conveyor and is the major reason that the Maritimes enjoy a relatively mild climate. More energy flows in the Gulf Stream than is carried in all the air patterns that pass over the Maritimes. It is the single largest source of energy, other than the sun, for the Maritimes and northern Europe.

Lately, researchers have noticed the Gulf Stream plays the "miner's canary" role in the world's climate. Miners used to bring caged canaries into the coal mines with them. The canaries were very susceptible to minute changes in the air in the mines, particularly methane or coal gas, a very dangerous and explosive gas found in all coal mines. When the canary died because of methane, miners knew it was time to leave, because even though the miners couldn't notice the changes in the air, the canaries did. In the same way, climatologists and ocean researchers are beginning to understand that changes in the Gulf Stream are harbingers of much greater and unnoticed changes in the pattern of the larger Ocean Conveyor and what is happening to the world's climate.

When the warm saline water of the Gulf Stream reaches the Arctic and cools, it creates a great mass of sinking, cold, salty water which helps draw more warm, salty tropical surface waters northward to replace the sinking waters. This is called thermohaline circulation. The study of this phenomenon has been going

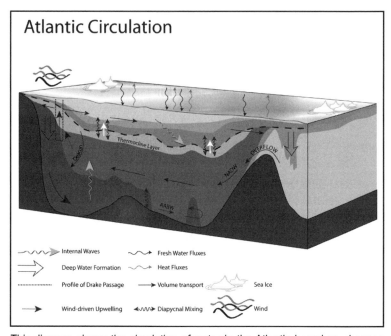

This diagram shows the circulation of water in the Atlantic based on changes in density, which in turn is based on temperature and salinity (thermohaline) differences in water masses.

on for decades, and it is recognized as a primary force driving global ocean circulation.

If the Ocean Conveyor were to shut down or slowed because of changes in temperature or salinity the results would be catastrophic. The entire North Atlantic, according to the latest computer models, would cool by three to five degrees Celsius and would make the mini ice age during the Middle Ages seem like a picnic. The winters in Atlantic Canada would be worse than any experienced in the past 5,000 years.

Is this just a theory? Has this ever happened before? There have been past conveyor shutdowns. And they have led to not only frigid winters and cool summers but also have been linked with widespread droughts around the rest of the world.

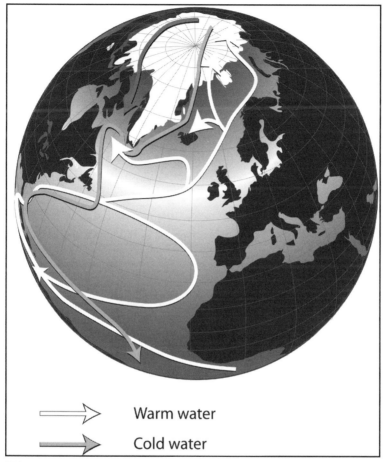

This diagram shows the various flows of currents in the North Atlantic. The surface currents are the white line and the deeper currents are the darker line.

What does this have to do with global warming? This is the "canary" part. With the great Greenland ice sheet melting faster than ever and at increasing rates, the amount of fresh water now streaming into the North Atlantic is disturbing. This fresh water is less dense than the saltier water from the Gulf Stream. It rides up over the salty water and keeps it from releasing its heat into the atmosphere. Without this cooling and the subsequent sinking there would be no driving force behind the conveyor and it could shut down. The result could be an almost immediate flip to cooling in the North Atlantic, an incredible paradox because all this would happen in spite of the fact that the rest of the world continues to heat up because of global warming.

This has been building up for a long time. We know the Greenland melt has changed the salinity of the North Atlantic over the past 40 or 50 years, but the change has been especially profound in the past decade, the largest changes ever recorded.

It is impossible to state if and when the Ocean Conveyor will slow or even shut down, but there are signs of a possible slowdown. In 2001, *Nature* magazine reported that the flow of cold, dense water from the Norwegian and Greenland Seas into the North Atlantic has diminished by at least 20 percent since 1950.

Two possible scenarios are being considered for the immediate and near future of the conveyor. The first is that the conveyor slows down within the next 20 years. Shipping, fuel, manufacturing, lifestyle and a host of other normal activities that we take for granted would all have to be adjusted and in some cases abandoned as a mini ice age, and possibly the onset of glaciation, takes place.

The second scenario is that the conveyor slows down a century from now and in the intervening years acts as a buffer to the general global warming occurring around the world. Our general climate in the Atlantic region and western Europe would not be too much affected. In such a scenario, if and when the conveyor restarts, global warming would accelerate and catch up to the changes that have occurred in the rest of the world. It is not yet certain which of the scenarios will play out or if there are other possibilities that have yet to be considered.

Will it launch us into a regional ice age where much of Europe and eastern North America will freeze as the Gulf Stream is shut down, while the rest of the world continues to have an increase in average temperature due to global warming? Or will global warming continue in spite of the melt?

El Niño/La Niña

Over the past 30 or 40 years meteorologists have been learning a lot about a couple of dramatic climate phenomena over the Pacific that affect the weather and climate of North America. These twins are called El Niño and La Niña and mean Christ Child in Spanish because they occur near Christmas. Normally El Niño and La Niña are officially defined as sustained sea surface temperature anomalies greater than half a degree Celsius across the central tropical Pacific Ocean. El Niño is a warming of the Pacific waters and La Niña is a cooling. If it is greater than normal it is an El Niño, or a warming of the water, and if it is cooler then it is called La Niña.

In Canada, their effects are profound and surprising. It is hard to believe that something like a warming or cooling of water thousands of kilometres away in the Pacific could affect the weather in Halifax or Moncton.

Generally, El Niños affect weather in the Maritime Provinces far more than do La Niñas. Because 2006 was a strong El Niño year most of North America experienced a milder than normal winter in 2006-07. Winter was late in onset (mid-January) and lasted only until mid-March in most of the Maritimes. Snowfall and precipitation amounts were below normal. NOAA, the National Oceanographic and Atmospheric Administration of the United States, declared the winter of 2006 the warmest on record globally.

Since 2006 was a strong El Niño year, the predicted very active hurricane season turned out to be much more average, after a record year for the 2005 season. In early 2008 it appeared that the La Niña phenomenon was gearing up with colder than average temperatures being measured in the Pacific. This is likely to be followed by a cold hard winter right across North America and a resurgence in hurricane activity in the Caribbean and Atlantic north of the equator, with more frequent and stronger than normal storms expected to plague the Atlantic in summer 2008.

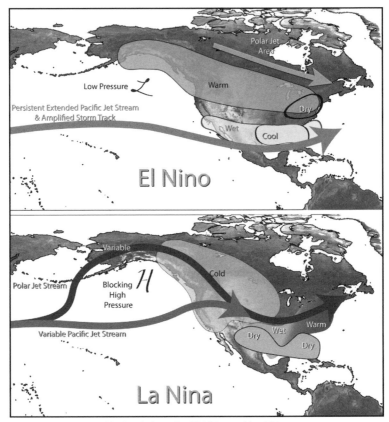

Air circulations for El Niño and La Niña.

In years during the El Niño event, the air pressure over India increases and falls over the central and eastern Pacific. The trade winds in the south Pacific weaken and warm air rises near Peru, which causes rain in the deserts. This results in rainfall in areas that are normally dry and brings drought to eastern areas.

Generally, during the El Niño event there is increased rainfall, storms and flooding in North America. Drought in Australia is also increased and it becomes drier and hotter in the Amazon. In eastern North America the winters become warmer and drier, while the west coast tends to be wetter and cooler. An upside to the El Niño is that during the Atlantic hurricane season the number and severity of hurricanes are reduced. In 2006 we saw a dramatic drop in hurricanes from the previous record-setting year.

The underlying causes of what motivates the El Niño are still not well understood. The general consensus, though, is that we can expect the El Niño to be enhanced as global warming progresses. During a La Niña event the Atlantic tropical cyclone activity is generally increased. La Niña also increases the severity of the North American winter, making it colder and longer. The La Niña condition often follows the El Niño, especially when the El Niño has been strong.

Extratropical Storms and Tropical Furies

In Canada, especially in Atlantic Canada, we have not had the great plague of hurricanes that happens with alarming regularity from May to November in the Caribbean and the southeastern United States. On average over the past 100 years there are ten to fifteen tropical storms each season, and three to seven that qualify as hurricanes. In recent years the number appears to have increased and 2005 was a record year. However, there is a new kid on the storm block that has merited some study. It brings together the fury of the hurricane and the longevity of the North Atlantic cyclone. It's called the Extratropical Transition Storm or ET.

Extratropical storms have been around for as long as there has been weather, but the mechanism that created them was not understood and it also appears that they were not as frequent. They are of particular concern to the Maritime region because of the way they form. It is now known that many of the hurricanes that do find their way to the North Atlantic waters and eastern Canada get a new life by becoming ETs.

An ET is a storm that gets its energy from the difference in air temperature rather than from warm ocean water. A hurricane's energy source comes from the warm ocean water and the cycle of rain that accompanies it. It's a positive feedback loop. The warmer the water, the greater the potential energy, which creates massive rainfall, which in turn puts more heat or energy into the storm, which drives the winds. Once the hurricane runs ashore or enters cooler waters it loses its energy source and the storm rapidly dissipates and dies. But if a hurricane runs into a much colder air mass, the temperature difference between the colder air and the moist tropical air strengthens the storm and gives a massive energy boost. The storm widens out, becomes larger and accelerates and the range of its winds broaden. When this happens the hurricane is said to have gone extratropical.

As the number of hurricanes increases, inevitably more find their way into North Atlantic waters to threaten the Atlantic Coast of Canada. In late September 2003, Hurricane Juan was a category one, verging on category two, storm that made a direct hit on Halifax and cut a swath through the province before hitting Prince Edward Island, causing $200 million in damages and killing four people.

The busiest hurricane season ever in the Atlantic was 2005, with many of the storms grazing Atlantic Canada. Four category five hurricanes – Emily, Katrina, Rita and Wilma – struck, the first time that more than two were recorded in one Caribbean season. Hurricane Katrina reduced New Orleans to a swamp and took more than 1,000 lives in the city alone. In 2006 and 2007, the Pacific La Niña reduced the numbers significantly, but those that did materialize were monsters.

It is expected that as climate change advances, the conditions become more favourable for hurricanes to morph into ETs. Cold fronts, the leading edges of drier Arctic air, are more likely to come in contact with hurricanes and change the primary energy source of the hurricane from warm tropical water to the difference in temperature and moisture content of the air.

3

The Problems

Human Population

It is easy to see from the table on page 72 that the human population on Earth has increased incredibly over the past 10,000 years. More people have lived in the past two centuries than in the preceding 98 centuries. Today there is no other species of animal on Earth, close to the size of humans, that has a population even remotely as large as ours, agricultural animals for our needs and consumption excluded.

The size of the human population is a problem on several levels. People require a place to live and the resources of the Earth on which to live. The total land area of the Earth is approximately 150 million square kilometres. The population total is 6.5 billion people. Roughly speaking, there are on the Earth today 38 people for every square kilometre of real estate. The oceans' area is approximately twice that of the land area, but so far we do not yet have the technology to populate the oceans.

Year	Population	Events
8000 BC	5,000,000	Advent of Agriculture/Cities
1000 BC	50,000,000	Egyptian/Assyrian Empires
500 BC	100,000,000	Persian/Qin Empire
1 AD	300,000,000	Roman Empire
1000	310,000,000	Islamic/Mongol Empires
1750	791,000,000	Spanish Empire
1800	978,000,000	British Empire
1850	1,262,000,000	European Colonial Empires
1900	1,650,000,000	British Empire at Height
1950	2,518,000,000	American Empire
1955	2,755,000,000	Soviet/American Tensions
1960	3,021,000,000	Space Race
1965	3,334,000,000	Vietnam War
1969	3,692,000,000	Moon Landing
1975	4,068,000,000	First Oil Crisis
1980	4,434,000,000	Home Computer Age
1985	4,830,000,000	Soviet Afghan War
1990	5,263,000,000	Soviet Empire Declines
1995	5,674,000,000	First US/Iraqi War
2000	6,070,000,000	Taliban/El Qaeda
2005	6,453,000,000	Second Iraqi War

In Nova Scotia the total population is just under a million and the area is 55,000 square kilometres. It has a ratio of about 18 people per square kilometre. New Brunswick has an area of 73,000 square kilometres, with a density of about 12 people per square kilometre. And Prince Edward Island has an area of 6,000 square kilometres with a density of 23 people per square kilometre. The Maritimes have an area of 134,000 square kilometres and a total population of about two million with an average density of 15 people per square kilometre or 7 hectares of land per person to live on and share with the entire ecosystem and the industry of people.

As far as the atmosphere is concerned, the total volume on the Earth is 3.3 billion cubic kilometres. That makes approximately 2.5 people per cubic kilometre of air or an area of 150 metres by 150 metres stretching from the ground to outer space for every person on Earth. But that also includes the ocean area. If you only talked about land area your space would shrink by two-thirds – to about 85 metres by 85 metres. In that volume of air, everything necessary for life on Earth – including your breathing, your share of all the industrial exhaust, all the animals, plants and microbes on the Earth – would have to make do.

Sounds pretty tight, doesn't it? Especially sharing the planet with our industry and all the creatures that also live here.

And the population is growing. And so is industry. Every emerging nation wants what the Western world has.

Ten thousand years ago, with just five million humans on the planet and no industry to sustain us, our ecological footprint was tiny in comparison to today's. Yet even then we had an impact. Those five million human inhabitants were able to eradicate the large ice age mammals, mammoths, mastodons, cave bears, wooly rhinoceros, large cats and to substantially reduce the numbers of many others. And the incredible fact is 1,000 years ago the population was 1,000 times less than it is today.

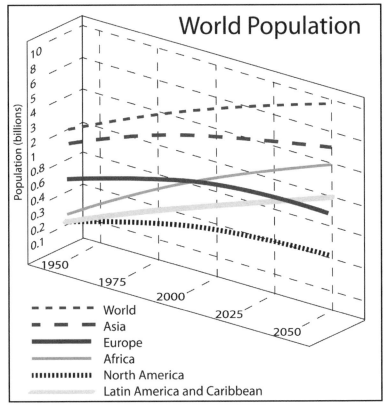

Population increases since 1950.

The latest estimates say that each year the human population increases by 75 million people, more than twice the total population of Canada. Put another way, every second more than two babies are born.

While it appears that Europe's numbers have stabilized and have begun to fall, Africa, Asia and the Americas all still have positive trajectories. It means that the total population of the Earth will be somewhere around ten billion before it begins to fall. Even if all the world adopted a birth rate of two per family, the population would continue to grow for another 25 years before levelling off because children being born today would reach parenting age in 25 years and add to the numbers.

> The Maritimes with its two million people is roughly equal to the Democratic Republic of Congo's 68 million in terms of population impact on the environment.

Not all populations are equal in eco-footprint. To quote George Orwell, "some are more equal than others" when we think of impact on the Earth and its ecosystem. In the Western world the average per capita consumption is about 30 times that of someone who lives in Africa. That makes Canada's 35 million inhabitants equivalent to Africa's nearly one billion.

> In the Maritimes governments, businesses and individuals have to work to create a new sustainable economic and population model that does not rely on growing populations to sustain services and our way of life. Every new mouth to feed in the Maritimes needs vast resources to live and grow, whether that person is born here or immigrates here, because of the ecologically expensive way of life.
>
> A growing population will only push us and the ecosystem to its limits more quickly than it would otherwise. We have already reached past our resources. Adding to the population because of economic concerns will only hasten the difficulties for our children and grandchildren. We don't have to look any further than the global ghettoes, which are the fastest growing segment of the entire human population. Each year, 80 percent of all new mouths to feed are born in ghettoes ... some 60 million, which in total consume what the Maritimes do today.

The hunter-gatherers of 10,000 years ago had to invent agriculture in order to survive because all the easy prey had been consumed and was extinct. The transition from hunter-gatherer had some surprising and unexpected results. It led to a human population explosion and in 8,000 years, some 100 human lifetimes, people went from five million to 300 million, an increase of 6,000 percent. It also led to massive population densities in entities called cities, which led to technologies, governments, armies, and above all, industry.

The population had begun to see the value of turning the environment into commodities. Our habitat footprint leapt to another order.

Habitat Footprint

To sustain our enormous population, we need room to live, room to create agricultural support systems to feed ourselves and room for the industry that takes the raw resources of the Earth, which we process to create what we want and need. This is called the habitat footprint or ecological footprint and the higher the population, the greater the footprint.

A quick comparison of life 10,000 years ago to life 2,000 years ago shows an incredible difference, probably the greatest shift in all human history.

Homo sapiens, our species, along with a number of other hominids, first appeared about 200,000 years ago during the peak of the previous ice advance. For the first 190,000 or so years we were hunter-gatherers. None of the hominids or humans appeared to have affected the ecosystem to any great extent. In fact, it is theorized that during one cataclysmic volcanic event in Indonesia about 75,000 years ago all hominids (Neanderthals and offshoots of Homo Erectus were just a few) and nearly all humans became extinct. Toba erupted with such force that it altered the climate of the Earth by ejecting an estimated 3,000 cubic kilometres of dust into the atmosphere. This was catastrophic to humans, and their numbers are thought to have plummeted to less than 10,000 individuals.

As a result, new niches opened and the survivors expanded across Africa, Europe, Asia, into Australia and finally across the Bering Strait into North and then South America. During this expansion, after Toba's eruption, humanity appears to have been responsible for the mass extinction of the great ice age mammals. By the time we come to the earliest clusters of humanity, called cities, in Mesopotamia, Egypt, India, China and Asia Minor, life has dramatically evolved to a different plane. Nature is still vastly unaffected, but a threshold has been breached. Through the technology of agriculture humanity has been able to launch itself on a trajectory that will employ technology in ever increasing scales to mold the ecosystem into a subsystem of humanity.

In the Maritimes the first peoples arrived some 12,000 to 15,000 years ago, just as the ice was making its rapid retreat and newly exposed land became habitable. Before the arrival of the Europeans 500 years ago, there were probably 20 million people living in North America. In the Maritimes, the population estimates range from 50,000 to 75,000. Most lived in small villages of interrelated groups that subsisted in a combined hunter-gatherer and early agriculture environment.

In 2,000 years this technology, a synthesis of agriculture, cities and industry allowed the population to explode from 300 million to more than 20 times that and on its way to 30 times before levelling off.

There is a tendency to think of our agricultural processes as a part of the natural framework of the Earth and the ecosystem. But, in fact, agriculture is now an industry no different than the computer or automobile industry. There is no more place, figuratively and literally, for the indigenous and wild creatures and plants of the world within the agricultural framework than there is for a tiger on the floor of a General Motors assembly plant. Agriculture has followed the technological trend of every other industry of humanity to its natural business conclusion where anything that inhibits the efficiency of its stated goal is culled, excluded and destroyed. Whether it is wild animals which forage in the displaced lands or opportunistic plants and fungi, the attack from agribusiness is swift and brutal.

In the Maritimes our per capita footprint is among the largest in the world, according to the Global Footprint Network. We have about 7 land hectares per person, but consume the resources of 11 hectares per person.

Globally, when we consider all the land available to all the people of the Earth as though we were distributed evenly with equal resources, the average is 2.5 hectares per person. That means if everyone on Earth consumes as much as Maritimers do we would need another four Earths to exist. That makes us at least four times the consumers we should be, if we want to share the planet's resources equally with every other human being on the planet. This is not a sustainable rate as species would become extinct because of our needs.

To create a footprint that is sustainable, where other creatures can also live, we would have to consume far less. In the Maritimes, our population density is lower than the global average but our land does not produce enough to sustain us at the rate of our current consumption. And our consumption is increasing. It has grown some 10 percent per decade over the past four decades.

In our cities we have had to install transportation grids for the services and goods that we consume to efficiently reach their markets. When populations were relatively low this did not present much of a problem. Early cities varied in size, with the famous Mesopotamian centres of Ur, Uruk, Lagash and Kish hovering in the 10,000 to 50,000 range 5,000 years ago. They had a small ecological impact and the agriculture and associated industry needed to sustain them could be placed close to the cities. But as the population grew, the need to acquire secure land area to sustain the city grew dramatically, as did the structural layout and the technology employed to achieve that goal. By the time Babylon was a force some 2,500 years ago, its population required the subservience and resources of an entire country. It was the first city to reach 250,000. Rome 500 years later, during the time of Christ, was a city of a million and required an empire to sustain itself. By the time it was in its heyday all the trees of Greece had been processed to build navies, houses, walls and burned for fuel; the fabled cedar trees of Lebanon were just a distant memory in the *Epic of Gilgamesh.*

We ship, in and out, vast amounts of resources and expand our reach with each passing year. Our climate, standard of living, industrialization and natural resources make Canada in general, and the Maritimes in particular, high consumers of the ecosystem. Canada ranks among the very highest in consumption of the world's resources, only behind the United States in per capita estimates. In general, European countries and Japan are much further ahead and are beginning to stabilize their consumption, though pretty much all the Western world consume far more than their share and many times more than the poorest nations in the world.

Transportation and Small Engines

To sustain our way of life we rely heavily on the resources and goods that come in from other parts of the world. From food, to the clothes we wear, the cars we drive, the planes we fly and the materials we use, we rely on the transportation system.

But transportation is not only used to service the technological civilization we have created, it is now also part of our recreation. Tourism, which in a few decades has grown enormously, is now a global enterprise.

Transportation accounts for more greenhouse gases emissions than any other human activity. In Canada, just personal transport accounts for 30 percent of the total emissions. If we factor in transportation for agriculture, tourism and recreation it is even more daunting. The total CO_2 emitted by internal combustion machines is many times larger than the amount of energy needed to heat and cool our homes.

In the West the transportation eco-footprint is expected to increase at the rate of 6 percent per decade. In developing countries trying to catch up to our standards of living it is much higher and problematic.

Our global economy, which has subsidized cheap fossil fuels, has given rise to the bizarre circumstance where it has been considered economically cheaper to cut our trees down in the Maritimes, ship them halfway around the world to China for processing and then ship them back to market in Nova Scotia, New Brunswick and PEI than it is to mill them at home. Until very recently, the environment and the social/human cost were never included in the equation.

In recent years there has been a marked shift to larger minivans, SUVs and other small trucks for basic transportation needs. The SUVs and other larger personal vehicles will on average remain in use for at least a decade. Add to that the fact that the number of vehicles on the road per family continues to rise steadily. Without a change, these factors make certain that our greenhouse gas emissions will remain high for the lifetime of these vehicles and beyond.

Our addiction to the automobile and travel has meant that even when more fuel-efficient vehicles have been introduced and used, the savings are mitigated by the rising number of kilometres travelled and the increased frequency of automobile use. Each year the number of kilometres travelled increases no matter what the price of fuel.

We add 70 million new cars to the nearly billion on the roads of the world each year. This new addition is larger than the total number of any species of large mammal on Earth, other than those we use for food. It's a staggering number.

In cities, the total space given over to automobiles and trucks for roads, parking and servicing is just over 40 percent. So in addition to living space, our cities also need driving space. As the population density increases so does the amount of space that is necessary to feed ourselves and get goods and services to the city.

A city that grows and seeks to maintain its servicing with automobile and truck traffic faces a couple of realities to overcome. Neither is palatable. If a city chooses a higher density in its core and to grow vertically, this mandates taller buildings which in turn automatically increase the number of trucks and cars to service the high population density, leading to congestion. If the city can expand in surface area, the increasing sprawl and expansion again mandates expanding the transportation grid.

Halifax, the largest urban centre in Atlantic Canada, has a metropolitan population of just under 400,000 with almost 250,000 cars, trucks and automobiles on the road. The number grows at the rate of 10,000 per year. Almost 50 percent of the urban space is taken up by parking, roads, streets and businesses related to the car. In the three Maritime Provinces there are more than one million passenger cars on the road.

Rethinking the transportation grid becomes crucial to urban planning. Rail on average uses about 70 percent less energy per unit of weight transported, making it far more efficient than road transport. The wheels on a train are made of steel and run on steel tracks, which makes for very little resistance. Steel wheels and rails allow for greater weights to be transported, which means greater efficiency. Added to that is the fact that rail traffic travels at a constant speed and does not have to deal with the type of congestion experienced in road gridlock that wastes fuel.

And finally, though there are rail mishaps, rail experiences far fewer accidents than does road traffic.

> Rail, though much more efficient and eco-friendly, has almost disappeared from the transportation landscape in the Maritimes. Rail traffic in the Maritimes is part of the national grid to take products and people in and out of the region. While rail was very important to the people and industrial transportation grid in past decades, cars and trucks and the subsidies for roads and road repairs spelled the end of intra-Maritime rail traffic.

In terms of emissions, public transport by rail is vastly superior from a number of standpoints, socially, environmentally and in actual land space required. It is estimated that rail loads in terms of people-moving efficiency is 1,000 percent higher than the automobile, allowing for the movement of as many as 20,000 people per hour at peak rates. A single rail line used for high-speed people transport is equivalent to ten lanes of automobile/ truck traffic and at least that many times safer. The total land use is cut back by 90 percent and CO_2 emissions are also proportionately lower. Public transport by rail is very common in Europe and parts of Asia and very efficient. But in Canada and the United States, while once very common, passenger rail traffic is a shadow of what it was 50 years ago, in spite of its obvious advantages.

In many cities around the world surface trains, called trams or streetcars, usually powered by electricity, are very common and practical. Widely used around the world, streetcars are extinct in Maritime cities and have been replaced by diesel-powered buses. Underground rail or subways are found in only two cities in Canada, Toronto and Montreal.

Ship traffic is almost solely used for the transport of freight and rarely does anyone use a ship as a mode of regularly scheduled travel, other than recreational travel on cruise ships. Ship traffic is probably the most efficient mode of transport in existence. Though most ships are now powered by diesel, in total numbers and the air pollution created, their CO_2 output is a fraction of the truck and automobile sector.

The other major source of CO_2 emissions related to small gas engines is through recreation and task service. Snowmobiles, outboard motors on boats, lawnmowers, leaf blowers, snow blowers, chainsaws and a host of other small gasoline engines number in the billions and create a huge CO_2 output that per hour of run time produce twice as much pollution as do cars and trucks. One gas-powered two-cycle engine running for half an hour is the CO_2 equivalent of driving a small car 50 kilometres at highway speeds. Where cars and trucks operate on prepared surfaces, which allow for smooth rolling, almost all recreational vehicles operate under harsher conditions. Snowmobiles push through snow, boats navigate through water and ATVs contend with varying terrain and conditions. The efficiency of the internal combustion engine is at its best when operated at a constant speed. None of the recreational vehicles works under those conditions. Constant speed and conditions produce the least pollution and greenhouse emissions. Continuously accelerating or decelerating vastly reduces efficiency. Unfortunately, even if recreational vehicles had engines as efficient as those of the automobile, the conditions under which they are used would make them at least twice as inefficient.

In the Maritimes, it's estimated there are more than a million inefficient small two-cycle engines, used to cut trees, mow lawns, blow leaves and snow, and push motorboats, ATVs and snowmobiles. That, coupled with the increasing number of cars on Maritime roads and the growing mileage travelled per individual, means CO_2 emissions have been climbing and are likely to continue to climb.

In 1998 there were 14 million registered cars in Canada. The Maritimes' share would be just under one million. In 2005 it was estimated each and every car on the road averaged about 16,000 kilometres per year or 40 kilometres per day.

By far the least efficient and most expensive way of moving anything from one place to another is by airplane. What makes the aerospace industry even remotely possible is the immense amount of liquid hydrocarbons we have access to and the massive subsidies paid to the air industry through military development.

Much of flying takes place in the stratosphere above the troposphere, the layer of the atmosphere that begins on the ground and where almost all the weather happens. Commercial and military flights dump most of their CO_2 and other pollutants into the stratosphere, where it is much less likely to be scrubbed out of the atmosphere by rainfall. Planes deposit CO_2 in the upper atmosphere where it's many times more harmful to the climate than any cars or trucks, the worst form of ground transport.

The estimated 350,000 aircraft worldwide emit more than a billion tonnes of carbon dioxide into the atmosphere. One 747, the world's most used aircraft, in a twelve-hour flight will turn 200 tonnes of jet fuel into CO_2 and a host of other gases, most of them noxious and dangerous. On an average 747 flight, that is half a tonne of jet fuel per person on the flight, or 500 litres, what the average car will use in a month.

At any given time, one-third to one-half of all the aircraft in the world are in the air and more than 90 percent of all flights take place in the northern hemisphere. Even though the aircraft industry has produced more fuel-efficient and less polluting engines, the increasing number of aircraft and flights per person mitigates the potential savings.

Energy

The energy that drives our world is fossil fuel – coal, oil and natural gas. The petrochemical industry, which utilizes these fossil fuels, is the largest industry in the world. In addition to energy, virtually all our plastics, synthetic compounds and most of our consumer items come from the petrochemical industry. In

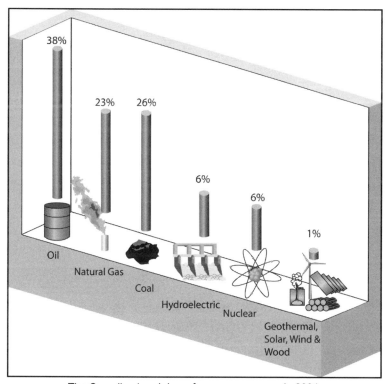

The Canadian breakdown for energy sources in 2004.

addition to fossil fuels, we have to add wood to the list as an energy source, though it is the Third World that uses wood as a primary source for heat and cooking.

Most of the world's electricity is generated from fossil fuels. The other forms of electricity generation include hydroelectric and nuclear, both of which produce no greenhouse emissions, but are much less available than fossil fuel electricity generation. For a variety of reasons, some of them to do with our climate, electricity is in great demand in North America. In the Maritimes the vast majority of power is generated by fossil fuels and in Nova Scotia coal-powered electricity is king.

Canada uses more electricity than India (520 versus 519 billion kilowatts per year) and the Maritimes use as much as the entire country of Columbia. Most of the available hydroelectricity has been tapped and there are few rivers close enough to major demand markets that have not already been harnessed to create hydroelectricity.

New Brunswick has the only nuclear power plant in the Maritimes. Tidal, wind, geothermal and solar power are an almost insignificant source of power in the Maritimes. While there has been a great deal of talk about developing clean energy, no meaningful initiatives have yet made any significant inroads.

Species Depletion

In the Maritimes many species have disappeared, or are on the verge of disappearance, because of human activity. The Blandings turtle, the piping plover, mainland moose, lynx, eastern cougar, wolf and black bear are dwindling in numbers as habitat destruction, human encroachment, hunting and changing environment take their toll.

Imported species, such as the starling and horned beetle, add another dimension to the pressures on indigenous species. The new species, either deliberately introduced by humans or brought into the region unknowingly, have no natural predators and are able to intrude on niches very successfully.

Freshwater smallmouth bass introduced for fishing have decimated salmon and trout populations. Carp, brought in as goldfish, sold in pet stores and released into the wild, actually change the water habitat to make conditions more favourable to themselves and less so for indigenous species.

The list of endangered and threatened species in the Maritimes compares in scope and severity to other threatened species around the world.

Our impact has made it difficult for us to coexist with the other species of the Earth. Biologists seem to be unanimous that there is a mass extinction occurring because of human activities. A 1998 survey indicated that in the next 30 years, if the current rates of extinction continue, 20 percent of all species we share the planet with will no longer be in existence. Edward O. Wilson, a famed American biologist and author, is more damning, suggesting that in 100 years 50 percent of all living creatures will be gone. (Wilson's books include *The Ants*, which won the Pulitzer Prize for Nonfiction, *Biophilia*, *The Diversity of Life*, and his latest, published in 2006, *The Creation: An appeal to save life on Earth*.)

One of the major groups of animals particularly threatened are the amphibians, which are dying off at an alarming rate all around the world. Amphibians, frogs, salamanders and toads consume insects that many other creatures find inedible or distasteful. They are also a crossover species from water to land and if they were ever to disappear from the world, Earth would lose a group of animals that were instrumental in the evolution of life.

Richard Wassersug of Dalhousie University has studied frogs and other amphibians. He's written many papers on the creatures, some detailing the interaction of amphibians and people and the threat they are under because of our activities. His studies, and those of other biologists, tell us we are wreaking havoc on the ecosystems on which amphibians depend.

Another study by researchers at Dalhousie is to count all the species of the oceans – in effect to do a census of what lives in the world's oceans. Chief scientist Ron O'Dor heads this ten-year effort to log all the species of the oceans, with an average of 50 new marine species being discovered each week. Scientists feel they have only skimmed the surface of what lives beneath the waves.

Oxygen Levels

Oxygen is undoubtedly the most important gas on Earth as far as life is concerned. Considering that it is also the second most reactive element in the periodic table and reacts with just about any other material around, it is remarkable that there is any free, unbound oxygen. In fact, it is what makes the Earth unique. Even though oxygen is the third most abundant element in the universe, because it is so reactive it is rarely found as a free gas outside the Earth.

So if oxygen is such a reactive element, how is it found on the Earth and is there for us to breathe?

For the past 600 million years, slightly more than the entire Phanerozoic era, oxygen has been a major constituent of the atmosphere and nearly 20 percent of the total mass or higher for the entire time.

It is interesting to note that if oxygen production by anaerobes and plants were to stop entirely tomorrow, in about 100 years all the free oxygen would be consumed through fires, respiration and oxidation processes and the levels would plunge to almost zero. So we should be grateful that plants and microbes are very busy keeping the oxygen content as high as it is.

The question becomes, why is 20 percent or so the magic minimum percentage and does it ever deviate from that? In fact, the level of oxygen has indeed fluctuated, rarely below 20 percent, but sometimes getting as high as 40 percent!

Over a span of time from roughly 360 to 240 million years ago, during the Carboniferous and Permian Periods, oxygen content in the atmosphere rose spectacularly. The Earth was in the midst of an ice age, not dissimilar to the current one that began 30 million years ago with the continent of Antarctica positioning itself over the South Pole. It seems the CO_2 content fell dramatically as the oxygen levels rose. At the same time that oxygen levels reached all-time highs and CO_2 levels fell, the greatest reserves of coal in the Earth's history were being deposited. The coal deposition rates were some 600 percent greater than at any other time. Somehow the carbon of the atmosphere was being taken out and transferred into the crust. With less carbon dioxide in the air, the Earth cooled, and yet somehow oxygen production jumped. The reasons, causes and effects are still being debated today and while no definitive, all-encompassing theories have been put forth that cover all the myriad of facts, we are very close to understanding the influences, causes and effects of rising and falling O_2 levels. It is very instructive to analyze that long past world and compare its conditions with ours.

What is certain is that this interesting mix of circumstances led to some pretty spectacular life. Some of these long gone creatures and plants can be seen today around the Bay of Fundy, at Joggins and Parrsboro in Nova Scotia. A walk along the fossil sites shows what the world must have been like at the height of an atmosphere flush with oxygen.

As the tides wear away the cliffs a veritable forest of fossilized cycads, ferns and club mosses become exposed with each twelve-hour rise and fall. What is amazing is that today these gymnosperms are all small plants, most just a metre or so tall. But 300 million years ago they were as tall as our tallest Maritime pines, some over 30 metres in height, with trunks half a metre in diameter. And the creatures that flew, crawled and lurked in these dank coastal forests were even more amazing. Dragonflies almost a metre in diameter darting between the trees, carnivorous, poisonous centipedes one and a half metres long chasing their prey, millipedes almost two metres long, snaking along rotting wood. At the top of the food chain were the amphibians, giant frog-like swamp denizens as big as pigs eating whatever was in reach.

Monsters all, compared to their modern day descendants. Why were they so large, especially the insects and arthropods, and what role did oxygen play in their size? In today's world they are limited in size by their ability to take in oxygen. They have neither lungs nor gills and rely on openings in their abdomens to diffuse the oxygen into their systems. Entomologists say this is the maximum theoretical size attainable. In today's 21 percent O_2 levels world, the largest insects are just around 100 grams in mass, but a higher O_2 environment would allow oxygen diffusion to be much more efficient and their subsequent size would increase dramatically.

During the Carboniferous Period it is thought that this indeed did happen and that insects and arthropods grew to gargantuan sizes, compared with today's comparatively diminutive offerings.

There are more clues to that ancient world to be found in Joggins, Nova Scotia. As you examine the sedimentary strata, layered and folded, along the shore, there are black layers running through the length of the strata. Some of the layers are coal seams and beds, but others are fossilized charcoal, the remnants of burned forests of that time. Because the oxygen content was so high, even coastal swamp forests were vulnerable to fire, and once started by lightning strikes, they would rage, even when wet, until the woody fuel was exhausted. In today's lower oxygen world such fires would be impossible, but in an oxygen-enriched environment, raging conflagrations could spring up from the slightest spark.

Some paleontologists think this is precisely why the high oxygen levels could not last. If the levels remained too high, fire was all too possible – even likely. Both the plants and the oxygen would be consumed and the CO_2 increased until the fires burned themselves out.

The decline in oxygen levels at the end of the Permian Period seemed to go with a rise in the CO_2 levels and the rise in global temperatures. What wasn't so obvious is why at the end of the Permian there was a catastrophic decline, in fact the worst decline, of species in the Earth's entire history.

The Great Dying is one of the greatest enigmas in paleontology. What, why and how this happened has occupied thousands of papers and many books and so far there isn't a "smoking gun" that definitively lays the blame on one cause. Here is what we do know. More than 90 percent of all ocean species and 70 percent of all terrestrial species died out in a period of time between the end of the Permian and the beginning of the Triassic. There seem to be two separate extinction events separated by as much as five million years. The worst volcanic eruption of the past 600 million years happened in what is now Siberia. There appear to have been two separate extraterrestrial impacts, one in Australia and one in Antarctica at least as big as the K-T (Cretaceous-Tertiary) asteroid of 65 million years ago. The climate had an abrupt and hot warming, greater than at any time in the past 600 million years.

Whether any or all of the listed facts created the Great Dying is now a matter of discussion. We do know it took the Earth millions of years to stabilize its climate and for life to recover.

It has been suggested that the impacts of the asteroids coupled with the massive volcanism (which may themselves be related) unbalanced the amount of CO_2 in the atmosphere, causing it to spike, heating the oceans dramatically, releasing methane hydrate, carbon dioxide and water vapour into the atmosphere, creating an almost runaway greenhouse effect. This in turn created even more heating and the addition of hydrogen sulfide, a notoriously dangerous poison, into the atmosphere, becoming the killer agent on land. In addition, oxygen levels fell to their lowest records in 600 million years, well below 20 percent.

While we have no asteroids looming that we know of, nor any supervolcanoes that are spewing forth magma at historic, continent-engulfing levels, we are changing the CO_2 levels on a scale not seen in millions of years. The oceans' top layers of water are also warming. The warming could mean the release of even more CO_2 as well as methane hydrate from the ocean bottom. Where the trigger point lies for this to happen is under more serious study. Once we reach 450 to 500 parts per million of CO_2 we are in uncharted climate territory.

If we trigger a warming period we may also harm our ability to produce the most important gas on the planet, oxygen. The widespread extinction of plants and creatures that produce oxygen would only exacerbate the overall catastrophe of runaway climate change.

Whether we are going to be responsible for another Great Dying is still well within the realm of discussion and conjecture, but that does not mean we should not consider the possibilities, especially in light of the fact that at least once in the Earth's past, life was almost ended through what was most certainly a dramatic shift in climate.

Rising Ocean Levels

By examining the past ocean levels we can get a good idea of what is to come. In the 110,000 years since the last interglacial the levels have changed by more than 120 metres, sometimes with amazing rapidity.

The rising ocean levels is due to two factors, the melting of the global ice caps and the thermal expansion of the water as it warms. There are three major questions: How fast is the thermal expansion? How fast is the Greenland ice sheet melting? How fast is the Antarctic ice sheet melting?

As the climate warms, both the thermal expansion and the ice melt are inevitable. It's just a question of how fast.

The Maritime coasts offer us an unparalleled view of the largest single entity on the Earth, our oceans. More than 80 percent of the Maritime population live within 20 kilometres of the ocean, and in Nova Scotia and Prince Edward Island the proportion is even higher. It is hard to understate the effect the oceans have on our lives.

Vulnerable areas in the Maritimes are across shallow low-lying areas, such as river mouths and marshes close to the ocean. Truro, Saint John, Moncton and much of Prince Edward Island are especially vulnerable to rising levels and floods. Every milimetre of ocean rise can translate to as much as a metre of erosion on shallow, wave-swept, sandy beaches.

As the ocean levels rise and storms become more severe, waves and storm surges will become more destructive. With an increase of one metre the most intense storms' high tides could create unprecedented floods. And with the floods there will be saltification of the land, so that when the storms do retreat and subside the damage would be virtually undoable, especially to agricultural lands.

Greenland

Greenland, the world's largest island, has the second largest ice sheet in the world after Antarctica. Its area is just under 2.5 million square kilometres and 90 percent is covered by glaciers three kilometres thick. When all or much of the ice melts on Greenland, as it has during every interglacial warming over the past two million years, the ocean levels rise by six metres globally and the Ocean Conveyor fluctuates wildly as a new climatic equilibrium is established.

But it's not all about rising levels and storms. We also have to consider the time factor. The rates of the melt are accelerating and the acceleration is accelerating. So even if the current rates do not inspire concern, the fact that rates are increasing exponentially should. During the end of the last glacial retreat, a mere 15,000 to 12,000 years ago, the ice melt rate in North America was phenomenal. Two glacial lakes were formed, Lake Missoula and the giant Lake Agassiz.

Lake Missoula was a prehistoric glacial lake in western Montana, about half the volume of Lake Michigan. It was created because of a 600-metre-high ice dam on the Clark Fork River. When the ice dam broke, it flooded the valleys of western Montana approximately some 325 kilometres eastward, not only once but many times.

The periodic rupturing of the ice dam resulted in the Missoula Floods, which swept across eastern Washington and down the Columbia River gorge approximately 40 times during a 2,000-year period.

Lake Agassiz was even more catastrophic. Climatologists believe that a major outbreak of Lake Agassiz in about 11,000 BC drained through the Great Lakes and St. Lawrence River into the Atlantic Ocean. A return of the ice offered a reprieve, and after retreating north of the Canadian border about 9,900 years ago it refilled. These events had a significant impact on climate, sea level and early human civilizations in the Younger Dryas Event.

The lake drained nearly completely over the next 1,000 years or so, leaving behind Lake Winnipeg, Lake Winnipegosis, Lake Manitoba, and Lake of the Woods, among others. The outlines and volumes of these lakes are still slowly changing as the Earth's crust continues to rebound from being depressed by the enormous weight of the ice.

If Greenland's now rapid and accelerating melting creates dammed lakes like Lake Missoula and Lake Agassiz, then they become time bombs for catastrophic releases of fresh water as the ice melts, with the capacity of releasing global climate-altering volumes of fresh water into the North Atlantic. The traditionally slow melt of the Greenland ice cap is now threatening to become a torrential melt as global warming increases.

If this should be the case, then the most affected region would be Atlantic Canada. The sudden rush of fresh water would have a radical reversal of the Gulf Stream, and Atlantic Canada as well as northern Europe would plunge into a rapid and very dangerous cooling, while global warming continued in the rest of the world until North Atlantic waters warmed.

Antarctica

With an area eight times that of Greenland and with an even thicker ice cap, Antarctica is the repository of 90 percent of the world's ice and 70 percent of all the world's fresh water. Its total volume of water, if all its ice caps were melted, would raise the global sea levels by an astounding 90 metres.

Antarctica has had permanent glaciers since it moved over the South Pole and interrupted the ocean currents that kept the Earth warmer some 40 million years ago. The Antarctic ice age has existed far longer than its northern counterpart.

The currents fed water to the ice caps of Antarctica and it went from subtropical to a permanently frozen wasteland. At the beginning of the Eocene Epoch, 55 million years ago, there were no permanent ice caps anywhere on Earth. But by its end the vast cycle of ice advance and ice retreat would begin, mostly in the southern hemisphere.

It would take another 30 million years before the currents of the north would be substantially changed by the widening Atlantic and the creation of the Himalayan Plateau, which would lock the northern hemisphere in its era of ice.

Over the past epoch and a small part of the preceding one (the Pleistocene and Pliocene), some three million years, the ice age at its greatest extent covered as much as a third of the entire globe's land area (the total global land area is roughly 145 million square kilometres); some 47 million square kilometres were under an ice sheet 1.6 to 3 kilometres thick. As the ice retreated in the north, liberating some 40 to 60 million cubic kilometres of water, raising the ocean levels 120 metres, the Antarctic remained, by and large, fast and frozen in ice. For the Antarctic, the ice age has lasted almost 40 million years without any let-up.

Since the extinction of the dinosaurs, the Earth on average has been getting colder. The exception has been the Paleocene Epoch and the beginning of the Eocene Epoch during what is called the Paleocene-Eocene Thermal Maximum (PETM). It is considered to be the warmest period of the past 65 million years. This was a time when the global temperatures spiked. The gradient or the difference in temperatures between the equator and the poles was perhaps half of what it is today. The world's oceans were warm from the surface to the abyssal regions. The poles were temperate to subtropical with extensive forests and no permanent ice at all. This thermal maximum lasted only 100,000 years. As it happens, it was also a time of great extinction. Many of the Earth's creatures died out yet again and though the event was not as big as the K-T (Cretaceous-Tertiary) Extinction that wiped out the dinosaurs, it was significant and dramatic.

Here is what makes this interesting. Today, as we enter a time of an almost runaway greenhouse effect, we are at risk of bringing on a change to the ice and the climate of Antarctica for the first time in 40 million years. Already huge cracks have begun to appear in the western Antarctic ice sheet and several huge ice islands have broken free in the past decade, something that is expected to become increasingly frequent as the climate of the Earth warms. Though it is not expected that much of the ice cap will melt this century, as the CO_2 levels approach 500 parts per million in the next 20 to 30 years, it is now impossible to say that the improbable will not happen over the next couple of centuries, plunging the entire Earth into a circumstance, climatically and ecologically, that has not been seen in more than 50 million years.

With 70 percent of the Earth's entire fresh water in its ice, tampering with Antarctica's climate is something that should be avoided at all costs.

4

What Works and What Doesn't

Human Population

China is famous for its imposition of one child per family birth control. And while the civil liberties organizations decry this abrogation of human rights, others applaud the attempt to limit the population of the most populous country on Earth. Today more people live in China than were on the entire Earth 150 years ago.

India is scheduled to surpass China in population some time in the next two decades. And while the populations of Russia and some European states have begun to decline, the world population continues to grow, especially in the underdeveloped nations of Africa, Asia and South and Central America.

Every year two more Canadas are added to the world population, more than two new people per second. The most critical threat to the globe today is from our runaway, exponential increase in population. At some point in the next 50 years it is expected the population will peak at somewhere between nine and twelve billion people. By that time much of the resources, arable land, species and food resources will be under threat even if the climate were not changing and adding to the crisis.

In addition, as the world modernizes and technology expands into Third World countries, the western economic model of consumerism is adopted. This increases the footprint of each person. In the West, one person is the equivalent of 30 to 40 people or one small village in Africa.

What has kept the West from addressing its contribution to the global crisis is its oft-stated need to keep its economic engine growing and expanding. It is said that our economic health is based on increasing markets, increased industrial activities and the utilization of all, of what is termed, natural resources to drive the economy. Most of the arguments against adopting policies for reducing global populations come from the economic sector. Politicians and big business tell us if they are forced to submit to environmental constraints, especially if there are limits imposed on the growth of population, then we risk economic collapse.

To bring the point home we can look at what were once the greatest fish stocks in the world, the famous Grand Banks off the coast of Atlantic Canada. In the 1950s fish scientists began to sound the alarm that at some point if the fishing wasn't curtailed the stocks would collapse irreversibly. Governments ignored the problem, questioning the scientists and their methodology. By the 1980s fish catches had fallen substantially, but we continued to ignore the problem. Fishing continued and within a decade the cod fishery, the once greatest fish resource in the world, one that had been fished for over 1,000 years, ceased and collapsed.

So far, in most countries the approach to the global human population is somewhat similar to our approach to the fisheries crisis. Politicians, governments and international business organizations generally think in short terms and that means whenever they can put the problem off to be dealt with by future generations that is precisely what they will do. As long as there is no immediate crisis affecting us at home we generally do not deal with it.

> The 2006 census shows the Maritimes to have a negligible population growth against the average of 2.6 percent yearly growth for the rest of Canada.

What adds to the complexity of the problem is that the issue of human population also has religious implications. All the main religions give people a free rein to make as many offspring as possible. In fact, it is a central tenet of the Christian Bible that humanity shall go forth and multiply. So, in addition to having to deal with the reality of a massive population burden, the world and those who would limit our population explosion have to deal with the fundamentalist interpretation, that it is our perceived God-given right to multiply without restriction.

> Even though the overall population growth of the Maritimes is the lowest in Canada and is not expected to increase much in the coming decade, there is a trend of increasing urban growth. Major centres such as Halifax – which has grown almost 4 percent over the past five years at the expense of smaller communities, has 40 percent of Nova Scotia's population and 15 percent of the Maritimes' – will continue to grow.

In the Third World, children are considered a resource to be exploited by the elders, who depend on their progeny to support them. The more children that parents have, the more likely they will have someone to look after them when they are too old to work. In the Third World there are no support systems or old age pensions or government programs that look after old people who can no longer work. Children become the support system and the retirement insurance. It's really not so different from the West's governments and businesses argument that without a young, growing population to support those who cannot work, especially the retired and aged, the economy will fail and chaos and social destabilization will follow.

The problem with that reasoning is at some point the population will push against the resources of the planet. There will be more mouths to feed and more land needed to house, support and maintain that growing population. And as the young population grows old itself, it will need increasing numbers of young to again support them and their needs in old age, and so on. It is again a positive feedback loop. At some point a threshold with be reached and the Earth will not be able to sustain the sheer numbers.

The idea of limiting population is unpalatable to politicians, especially when they have to confront the religious ethics of those who believe their right to procreate is divine.

In North America and Europe women have liberated themselves from archaic traditions and become educated. They are no longer seen as just servants and baby makers under the auspices of male demagogues, and birth levels have fallen. But the overall population rates have continued to grow, offset by immigration from the surpluses of poorer nations. However, there is a more sinister side to all of this and it lies in our consumer driven society.

Because the Third World has so many hungry mouths to feed, Western businesses have been quick to exploit the cheap labour and lack of environmental laws and protection by shifting production of consumer goods to the Third World, which we happily buy back.

The upshot is that while it appears we have made progress in dealing with the population excesses and cleaned up our own backyard, we have just shifted the burden to another part of the world, where the dearth of environmental regulation and human rights allows us to distance ourselves from our actions.

In the early 1800s Robert Malthus introduced the world to the concept of an end to unrestricted human population growth. The English demographer and political economist, who lived from 1766 to 1834, is best known for his pessimistic but highly influential views on population growth. He forecast there was a limit to the population that could be supported by Earth's ecosystems. He looked at food production as a linear growth function and the population as an exponential growth function. In his theories, he stated population growth would soon exceed the ability to feed ourselves. His prediction that our population would exceed our resources has not yet come to pass for a variety of reasons that he could not foresee during his lifetime. Our technology, especially agriculture and medicine, has given us a great cushion, making it possible to forestall the inevitable for the better part of a century. It has also allowed people to put on blinders to the limits of our technology. Without it many hundreds of millions and perhaps billions would suffer greatly.

> The Maritimes are expected to remain a slow population growth region for at least the next decade. According to the 2006 Canadian census, the Maritimes' population growth, reflecting the trend for the rest of the country, will increase mainly through immigration, since birth rates are below 1.5 per couple, well below replacement rates.

Because of our technological prowess many people now talk about the necessity of having a burgeoning population, just to support the technological advances we will inevitably make in the future to solve our problems. They say without the rapid and continued exponential growth of our population we will fail as a species, precisely because we will outstrip our resources and that the only hope we have is now based on increasing our numbers to push ahead the technology.

This line of reason is nothing if not perilous. It is putting us in a headlong rush toward disaster. We depend on the ecosystems and the millions of creatures and the environment in which we live. To think it is expendable and that our technology can supplant the environment to save us is the height of folly. This approach fails to consider the creatures with whom we share the planet and treats them as fodder for our consumerism. No matter how technological we become, we are still the product of the Earth's environment, which is the basis of all life. We are inextricably bound into the matrix of the world and to think that in a few short centuries we could discard and supplant it is indeed risky beyond belief. Assuming we could deal with the morality of churning the environment and ecosystem into technological pulp, this self-centred approach has very little room for error. Once we go down that path there is no turning back. At some point we will pass a point of no return and if our technology fails us, there will be no support from the ecosystem.

There are some who even think that if we can survive the next 50 or so years technological breakthroughs loom ahead that will lead us to thousands of years of nirvana. They point to the advent of nanotechnology, computers, gene therapy and self-replicating systems, which will allow humans to transcend their mortality. In this brave new world people become the equivalent of gods, living forever and even populating the galaxy and beyond. The futuristist Ray Kurzweil has written a book, *The Singularity is Near: When Humans Transcend Biology*, about this perceived rosy future where technologies transform people into gods. While it is interesting to speculate on what might or might not be, in this new century the stark reality is most people live not the way that we do in the West, where 20 percent of the world consumes 80 percent of the world's resources, but in a world where the majority of people are born into what is the fastest growing segment of human society, the urban slum. All around the world four out of every five babies born take their first breath and their last within the confines and detritus of the garbage and environmental desolation of these desolate landscapes. Even though only 20 percent of humanity lives in slums, slum birth rates are much higher than in non-slum regions.

The world's largest slum is in Mumbai (according to Mike Davis in his book *Planet of Slums*), formerly called Bombay, the most industrialized and technologically advanced city of India, home to Bollywood, computer software companies and a burgeoning middle class. Mumbai has a total population of about 20 million and is expected to be close to 30 million in the next decade. India's 2001 census estimated the population of the Mumbai slum is near seven million. Those who make up the pinnacle of Mumbai's society do so at the expense of the 60 percent who live in slums, sift through the mountains of garbage and live within the most appalling circumstances. And Mumbai is not an isolated case. Dozens of cities around the world, including some in the West, have slums. Slums are the fastest growing segments of human society. South and Central America, Africa, and many Asian cities groan under the weight of their poverty.

And while we in the West dream of spaceships, intelligent computers and evolving past the environment, the reality, the indescribably sad reality, is that we are still bound to our planet and its resources and far more people are doing with less and less.

What is the solution? Quite simply we need to reduce our population now. We need to plan for the reduction. We need to examine our dependence on technology and use technology not as a springboard for increased sales and marketing goods, but to reduce our eco-footprint.

Energy

Energy is what separates the haves from the have-nots. The West has corralled the bulk of the world's most accessible and powerful energy source: fossil fuels, especially oil. Though we have been making use of fossil fuels for centuries, it is only in the twentieth century that oil really became the energy source of choice. Oil has transformed our transportation, homes, industry and technology.

Coal is the most accessible and abundant of all the fossil fuels. It presents another daunting problem because it is the dirtiest in terms of pollution and GHGs. Now that both India and China have become industrialized and have powered their industrialization with coal, the problem has become even more acute.

Nova Scotia, like the United States, relies on imported fossil fuels for most of its electrical power. The offshore natural gas fields are in decline and no new sources have been found, so to add to our carbon footprint, Nova Scotia imports fuel from Venezuela and Russia.

Because of the amount of energy that has to be generated to keep the industrialized world powered, fossil fuels are both the solution and the problem. Whether it is wood, ethanol, gasoline, natural gas, methane, coal, peat or any of the other variants of hydrocarbons, they all create CO_2. Because of the number of people and the enormous size of our industry, our energy needs are overburdening the ecosystem.

If we continue to burn hydrocarbons for energy, CO_2 has to be kept from getting into the atmosphere. It's called CO_2 sequestering. Some have suggested we pump CO_2 into the ground into played-out oil fields to provide pressure to force the oil to the surface. Once the oil has been completely exhausted the well is capped and the CO_2 is sealed in the ground.

The problem is no one knows whether the CO_2 will eventually find its way back to the surface and present a greenhouse gas hazard or whether the gas will remain in the ground. Initial indications are that because the oil wells are in sedimentary rock, the highly pressurized CO_2 eventually is absorbed by groundwater and makes its way back to the surface, where it leeches out into the atmosphere. In places where the water does not find its way to the surface, the water is acidified, dissolves much of the surrounding rock matrix and becomes toxified, presenting a threat to life in yet another way. Most of the tests to keep CO_2

from escaping into the atmosphere have either proven to have significant technological side effects or are so expensive as to make the process unusable.

Fossil fuels have the unfortunate quality of being relatively cheap (if you don't reclaim the waste) and plentiful, so it is only because of the vast amounts we use that they have turned out to be a plague on the world. The petrochemical industry is the largest industry in the world and our oil-based companies have enormous social and monetary clout. When combined with the automobile manufacturers they present a formidable foe to a new and cleaner energy lifestyle.

Oil and automobile industries have had a history of ignoring social and scientific realities, using questionable information and tactics to boost sales, and even circumventing and breaking the laws to get what they want.

Lead in gasoline is a perfect example. During the 1920s engine knock or pre-ignition became a significant problem in car engines as they became larger and more powerful. The problem almost spelled the end of the internal combustion gasoline engine in the automobile. It was discovered that lead could be added to the gasoline to boost the octane rating, which would eliminate the problem. But, as in many solutions, there was a price to pay for the new lease on life for the gasoline engine. The lead additive called tetra-ethyl lead or TEL was found to be extremely toxic. Many early researchers of TEL became ill and dozens died. Yet in 1924, DuPont and General Motors created the Ethyl Gasoline Corporation to produce and market TEL.

As it was burned in car engines the lead in TEL was spewed into the environment by millions of automobiles. Lead is a toxic element and especially affects the nervous systems of small children. We knew that back in the 1920s yet it took almost 50 years to end TEL use. In the US in 1972, the Environmental Protection Agency launched an initiative to end the use of leaded gasoline, which caused Ethyl Corp. to sue the EPA. The EPA won, so in 1976 the phase-out began and was completed by 1986.

Even though leaded gasoline is largely gone in North America, it has left high concentrations of lead in the dirt adjacent to all roads that were constructed during the years when lead was still in gasoline. Child development specialists now advise parents to not let their children play in such dirt, because lead-laced dirt can be ingested with catastrophic results.

Closer to home, we in the Maritimes must re-examine how power utilities and governments have justified, and continue to rationalize, the use of coal and oil to generate electricity as well as why we have allowed our public transit and rail systems to be dismantled and destroyed over the past few decades.

There are a number of routes we can take almost immediately in making electricity for general consumption. The technologies exist and have been developed and successfully implemented in other areas in the world. There are four technologies that come to mind immediately that could alleviate the need to consume oil and coal for electrical power.

Tidal power has wonderful possibilities, given the fact the most famous tides in the world are also the highest with almost limitless potential. Twice a day there are high and low tides, and millions of gallons of water spill in and out of the estuaries and inlets along the Bay of Fundy. These tides could provide a huge auxiliary boost to a main power grid. There is almost no downside to tidal power generation and it is one of the great mysteries to me why this has taken so long to be developed. It is just now being re-examined and a host of new initiatives appear to be underway. Whether these new initiatives succeed remains to be seen. The harnessing of tidal power could provide as much energy as the vaunted Niagara Falls of southern Ontario.

Wind power has been underutilized in the Maritimes. In Europe, wind has been a source of power for centuries and in Germany and Denmark, modern efficient turbines generate 15 to 20 percent of the total grid. Given that we in the Maritimes have an almost ceaseless wind driven by our weather systems and heat differential between the water and land, wind power is a natural and could be an excellent supplementary source of energy.

For example, Prince Edward Island has recently had eight new 660-watt wind turbines added to its North Cape Wind Farm and roughly 5 percent of the province's total electrical needs are met by wind turbines. Wind farms are now popping up all across the Maritimes with new turbines appearing in Pubnico and Cape Breton in Nova Scotia, and in the Kent Hills area of New Brunswick. The downside to wind power is it is not as continuous and not as reliable. There is also the problem that the revolving blades pose a hazard to birds and some people consider the turbines to be unsightly. In addition, some people and even animals appear to be sensitive to the low frequency vibrations of the turbines. Studies are now underway to determine the seriousness of these concerns.

Even though the Maritimes are not the sunniest area of the world we do get enough sunshine to make solar power a viable option as an energy assist on a small scale. Hot water heating, home heating and cooling, battery charging and a host of other small tasks make solar power, both passive and active, a very inexpensive and easy option. Remarkably efficient and reliable solar panels are now available for homes. There is a downside to solar panels, because there is still the problem of expense and toxic chemicals after the panels have served their function and are worn out. The materials have to be disposed of carefully and recycled.

Geothermal power (tapping into the underground heat of the Earth) in the Maritimes, though not as accessible and prevalent as in Iceland and other parts of the world, is a possibility that can be developed and used in parts of the region. Tests in some areas indicate that because of extensive mining and the depths and extent of the mines there is heat energy that can be tapped to heat buildings or generate electricity. Springhill, Nova Scotia, where mining was dominant for almost 100 years, has had limited success using geothermal energy. Springhill's Geothermal Industrial Park uses geothermal energy from the floodwater of the abandoned mines, which is at 18°C, to provide heat and reduce heating costs. A gravity circulation in a closed loop provides a virtually limitless flow of heat at an almost zero environmental impact. Natural Resources Canada says this is the first industrial site in Canada to demonstrate the economic and technical viability of geothermal energy.

These four quick energy fixes to get us to reduce the reliance on fossil fuel power generation are just the tip of the engineering innovations that could help reduce the fossil fuel emissions.

One of the more innovative projects in Halifax uses harbour water for air conditioning in some of the newer buildings. Because the deeper water is cool, around 13°C, engineers have devised efficient ways for it to be used as coolant for air conditioning the interiors of the buildings during the summer. Another project is pumping cold water into an underground sink to cool the rock during the winter and then use the cold to air condition buildings in the summer. Other ideas, such as using passive solar radiation during the hottest part of the day to heat bedrock beneath the buildings and then extracting it as needed, are also being researched.

It is estimated that if all three levels of government participated with incentives for industry to spur research, new and efficient green energy processes could reduce electrical needs from the central power generated by fossil fuels by 40 percent. Rather than be a cost, the push to make our power grid greener would be a source of revenue and jobs. The innovation is a technology that could be exported at a substantial gain to investors and stakeholders. The Maritime urban centres, especially Halifax, have a highly developed educational and research infrastructure and are close to major markets, which with a little support could become a centre for green energy innovation. All that is missing is the political will to drive the necessary investments to spur the research.

In order to get our emissions down, still have enough energy to live and not do more damage to the planet, we have to look at the whole energy picture and begin to re-evaluate our wants, needs and abilities and what this will mean. We also have to look at the information objectively and counter the inevitable torrent of misinformation and obfuscation by special interest groups whose sole objective is not to enlighten and assist, but rather to enhance their business and economic interests at the expense of the environment.

The re-examination of the way we live is crucial. Because we have advanced technology and scientific prowess what we do will have an enormous effect on what the developing nations will do. By developing energy efficiency we will also be helping the Third World, which means that we will reap those benefits as well.

The immediate goal has to be to reduce actual emissions right now. The bottom line is that because of fossil fuels, we continue, day after day, to throw greenhouse gases into the atmosphere.

Ultimately, the sources of energy listed above are stopgaps and temporary measures until entirely new technologies for energy generation come online that completely supplant fossil fuels and release us from their grip. The goal of the above technologies and secondary energy sources is not to solve the problem, but to end the dominance of fossil fuels and cut our emissions of greenhouse gases. Our energy needs will continue to climb and we need to stop the emissions immediately. These secondary energy sources, while not perfect, are much better and more efficient for all concerned than fossil fuels.

The ultimate, long-term goal is to find a clean, safe energy. An alternative, called the hydrogen economy, exists and is almost there. But there are hurdles that need to be solved to make it totally viable. In the short term, we need to begin with a series of small incremental steps. Over the long term, we need to develop a cradle-to-grave philosophy that doesn't treat the Earth and its ecosystem as a garbage dump. If we act now and change our thinking for the future, substantial progress that cannot be discounted will be made.

Transportation/Travel

It is impossible to speak of reining in climate change gases and not address transportation issues. The trend has been that as the urban centres grow around the world so does the use of the automobile and related truck traffic. The statistics speak for themselves. In the Maritimes, cars outnumber every species of large animal over 50 kilograms combined. The 1:2 ratio between cars and every man, woman and child in the Maritimes is a growing percentage. And this statistic does not include freight and business traffic.

As well as the number of individual cars, the average horse-power and fuel consumption of the vehicles driven in the Maritimes continues to rise. So even if cars become more efficient by a significant margin, their increasing numbers mitigate any potential gains in efficiency per vehicle.

Here is what we know. No hydrocarbon is clean. When burned it produces climate change emissions. Though emissions have gotten cleaner in terms of the particulate matter, the per kilometre tonnage of CO_2 emitted has increased, not declined. No matter how clean, all engines in commercial use today produce CO_2.

The car not only uses energy, fossil fuels, and emits a huge proportion of the total climate change gases during its operation, but the manufacture, repair and distribution of the automobile represent even more of a greenhouse deficit. In addition, the space cars take up in roads, streets and parking lots represents a huge energy deficit, since the asphalt and concrete detract from natural land with plants that could absorb the CO_2. More than a million tires per year find their way into Maritime disposal centres. And so far no effective method has been found to dispose of cars and their parts after the useful life of the car has ended. Some of the proposals involve the combustion of the materials that are burnable, but again this presents another significant source of CO_2 and other climate change gases.

The Maritimes do not manufacture any automobiles or

trucks and few of their parts. With the global economy and just-in-time inventories, where manufacturers rely on shipping rather than warehousing, every car and virtually all their parts and constituent material have to be imported as quickly as possible, again at significant cost to the environment, especially the atmosphere.

The great myth about the automobile is that there are efficient automobiles, now and in the near future. In terms of moving people from one place to another the car is the most inefficient surface mode of transport that we have and only exceeded by air travel in energy inefficiency. Even the smallest car represents a massive environmental footprint when compared with almost any other form of transport.

It is a sad fact that battling business interests can be thankless and difficult. Many battles are won, but more are abandoned because of the willingness of business interests and multinationals to litigate, tying up individuals and organizations who go against them for decades in expensive and exhausting legal battles.

Here is one example where the automobile industry, notably General Motors, won. We have been paying for that win ever since. The Great American Streetcar Scandal is detailed by Jim Motavalli in his 2001 book, *Forward Drive: The Race to Build "Clean" Cars for the Future*. In the 1920s, when 90 percent of Americans in cities travelled by trolley and streetcar, General Motors along with Firestone, Mack Truck, Standard Oil and others began a covert operation to undermine the urban rail system of the United States. Through a company called National City Lines (NCL) they succeeded in buying up publicly traded companies in 80 American cities, reducing the services to discourage users and campaigning for a nationally funded roads system to cater to the automobile and truck. By the 1950s the consortium had succeeded in decimating the public transit systems and has never looked back. Today our cities are dominated by automobiles and trucks and internal combustion machines. This loss has played a substantial role in shaping our lives, environments and now our planet.

An end to the culture of the personal car cannot happen without an entirely new approach to the transportation problem which is linked to our lifestyle.

Halifax Streetcars: The Nova Scotia Light and Power Company ran Halifax's distinctive electric rail streetcar system. It ran an all Birney fleet from the 1920s until its closure in 1949. There was only one streetcar loop in the system, so double-ended cars were a necessity. After that, electric trolley buses ran, in a rails-to-rubber conversion purchased from the US. By the late 1950s they were also phased out.

From the mid-1850s to the 1930s Nova Scotia and New Brunswick had numerous rail lines that linked almost every town and city to each other and to external points. Even in the 1950s rail dayliners ran to the Annapolis Valley and Yarmouth from Halifax. The systems were well used, running an extensive and economical schedule. But the 1950s saw increased pressure from the automobile manufacturers, trucking and fuel companies which led to massive government subsidies for highways, artificially low fuel costs and the squeezing of public purses for public transportation. By the 1970s the beginning of the end was in sight and by 1990 the rails were virtually defunct. Today most track has been torn up and the land converted to walking and recreation paths.

Despite improved fuel efficiency, annual energy use in freight transport increased 30.5 percent between 1990 and 1999, and nearly all of this increase was due to a 42.1 percent increase in energy used by the trucking sector. Excluding small and medium trucks, energy used by large trucks as a group increased 61.6 percent. Energy used by the rail freight sector declined 6 percent.

On average, large trucks (more than 14,970 kilograms) use 9.2 times as much energy as rail per tonne-kilometre. Intercity tractor-trailer trucks use five times as much energy as rail per tonne-kilometre. Between 1990 and 1999, trucking increased its share of freight traffic. It would be useful to investigate how the trend of shifting to trucking was influenced by government policies or other factors. The increase in freight energy used between 1990 and 1999 would have been mitigated if more freight had gone by rail.

It has been said that heavy trucks had greater gains in energy efficiency between 1990 and 1999 than any other transportation mode. This is because the truck sector had a bigger base of energy use in 1990 from which to squeeze efficiency. Large trucks had more energy intensity to shed.

Greenhouse gas emissions closely track the use of fossil fuels. Freight GHG emissions increased 29.7 percent between 1990 and 1999, and nearly all of this increase was due to a 43 percent increase in trucking GHG emissions. The shift in the freight market to trucking is working against policies to reduce GHG emissions, such as the Government of Canada Action Plan 2000 and the National Action Program on Climate Change.

It is important that any future GHG emissions trading system avoid penalizing modes such as rail and marine that are already energy efficient. Reducing a tonne of emissions by shifting freight to a more fuel-efficient mode should be worth as much as reducing a tonne of emissions by improving truck fuel-efficiency.

In the 1980s big box, US-style stores were introduced to cities in the Maritimes. Most of the big box stores were set up in the suburbs outside the core of the cities, necessitating the use of an automobile. Shoppers converged upon these stores. Smaller single store types of businesses could not complete on a cost basis and many failed.

As city cores have degenerated, families have flocked to the suburbs, which are set up to be serviced by the automobile. Mass transit is inadequate and schools, businesses, and recreation centres are substantial distances away, necessitating cars. As the suburbs become larger and more expansive, more land is converted from forest, field and stream to manicured lawns, roads and golf courses, which in turn decreases our ability to handle the increased CO_2 and other climate change emissions by the increased automobile traffic.

It appears that the root of the Western lifestyle is consumption, driven quite literally by the automobile and truck traffic. The more we are able to travel, the more we set up our lives to necessitate travel.

A bizarre offshoot of this need to travel is that travel itself has become a recreation. Snowmobiles, ATVs, jet skis, motor boats, motorized homes and vacations abroad have all in the past 50 years become a part of Western life. In centuries past only the wealthiest travelled. And of those who did, it was not usually as sightseers, but rather to look after colonial interests and exploit less technological cultures. Most travel in bygone years was done out of necessity. Virtually all of Europe's poor were motivated by starvation, war and persecution to find new homes.

Today's travellers take their wealth abroad as they recreate. In fact, the fabled "snowbirds" of Canada make yearly pilgrimages to Florida and California, where they have winter homes for substantial parts of the year. They have become a very important part of the southern winter economy.

> In total 200,000 Maritimers each year take a vacation in southern climes, 10 percent of the entire population. Just under 100,000 Maritimers travel to Florida each year to escape the winter cold, about 5 percent of the total population. Florida is the destination of 50 percent of Maritimers.

A report by the International Civil Aviation Organization (ICAO) stated that the number of international air passengers worldwide rose from 88 million in 1972 to 344 million in 1994. As a consequence, tourism now accounts for more than 60 percent of air travel and is therefore responsible for an estimated 7 percent of the total carbon emissions globally. This percentage is likely to rise considerably with the number of international travellers expected to increase from 594 million in 1996 to 1.6 billion by 2020.

According to the Natural Resource Defence Council (NRDC), fuel burned by jet planes puts nitrogen oxide and water vapour at 9,000 metres. These two additional greenhouse gases together give as much as twice the global warming effect as the carbon dioxide released by the plane.

Marine Travel and its Effects

The absolute hands-down winner in the energy efficiency sweep-stakes is the ship. Depending on size and configuration, ships are up to ten times more efficient than rail. And if they use sails and solar panels to augment the traditional diesel engines, the efficiency for moving people and cargo is outstanding.

There is an economic downside the Maritimes have to consider as the world goes to low energy use trans-portation. As businesses realize the benefits and potential profits in shipping on water, it becomes good business to make ships as large a part of the transportation equation as possible and limit other more expensive forms of trans-port. That means that deepwater inland ports become increasingly sought after to penetrate as efficiently as pos-sible the heartland and central North American markets.

The Maritimes are particularly vulnerable to being bypassed, even though they have great harbours, be-cause Montreal and Quebec City present substantial energy efficiencies. Cities in the Great Lakes region also represent a threat, though climate change is already causing substantial lowering of lake levels, taking its toll on shipping. Ports along the US eastern shore with better service and rail connections have already bitten into ship-ping in Halifax.

As far as total overall environmental effects are concerned, we have a number of very serious issues that must be resolved to make ships the best form of transport. Much of the world's commodities is now carried by superlarge container ships and tankers. These ships dwarf anything that was afloat even 30 years ago. And as the size of these ships continues to grow the amount of cargo carried grows. As a result, even one marine mishap can have devastating consequences, especially if the cargo is something like crude oil that can kill untold species of animals and poison beaches and water. Even a relatively low rate of mishap still creates a large impact on an increasingly fragile ecosystem.

In addition to the risk of spills we have to consider the direct effects of just the operation of these ships. Many sea mammals, especially whales, are killed by colliding with these giant monsters. Marine shipping lanes have a catastrophic effect on these creatures.

These ships travel around the world and bring unwanted hitchhikers with them. When ballast water is improperly discharged, invasive and highly destructive imported species of plants and animals – such as zebra mussels, eels and lampreys – wreak havoc on ecosystems. This continues to happen with increasing frequency. Species are able to hitchhike on cargo as stowaways. The longhorn beetle now plaguing Maritime forests is a perfect example of a pest making its way from Asia to North America via wood products on cargo ships.

Once a new species is introduced to a new habitat, it is virtually impossible to eradicate. In fact, no introduced species, once it makes a successful beachhead, has ever been eradicated. The list is daunting and gives an idea of the potential harm; it includes the starling, the spruce budworm, cats, rats, lamprey eels, pigs, rabbits and the African bee. The introduced species has no enemies and, multipling at will, soon pushes out indigenous species.

Military Flying

The discussion about travel would not be complete without a short diversion into the military use of air travel. Most of the data available on the military's consumption of energy and materials comes from the United States. Indeed, with a military machine of unparalleled proportions, it is not surprising that the US armed forces consume astronomical quantities of energy and materials.

The Pentagon (through the military) is considered the single largest domestic consumer of oil in the US. It is very likely the largest worldwide. The Department of Defense purchased 200 billion barrels of oil for military use in 1989 – enough to run all of the US public transit systems for 22 years.

In less than one hour an F-16 consumes almost twice as much gas as the average American motorist during one year. A modern battle tank's fuel consumption is so high that it can be measured in gallons per kilometre. The Pentagon uses from 5 to 15 percent of the US non-fuel minerals.

The global statistics on the military's consumption of energy and materials are equally sobering:

* approximately one quarter (42 million tons per year) of the world's jet fuel is used by armed forces;

* armed forces consume 9 percent of global iron and steel;

* the worldwide military use of aluminum, copper, nickel and platinum is greater than the entire Third World's demand for these materials.

As much as 70 percent of all airspace is used for military purposes in the United States. The majority of military flights take place over the western US. There are approximately 90,000 training sorties per year and one-fifth of these are at very low levels.

Canada has one of the world's most extensive airspaces for military purposes. Over 100,000 square kilometres were assigned to the Goose Bay Air Base in Labrador, though that has been discontinued. The Cold Lake Air Weapons Range low flying area stretches over 660,000 square kilometres (from British Columbia to Manitoba), 6.6 percent of the national area.

While Canada's military is dwarfed by that of the United States, as a partner of the US and NATO, a substantial amount of American military activity takes place over Canadian air space. Halifax is a major military centre in Canada as is CFB Gagetown in New Brunswick. Though there are no statistics available for the amount of fuel burnt for military exercises, it is probably safe to assume that a significant portion of climate change emissions comes from the military.

Reuse, Recycle and Reduce: Does This Work?

The idea that we can reuse, recycle and reduce our way to planetary health is a myth. Our energy consumption is so high in the West because we have a consumer society. We measure our successes by the number of possessions we have and acquire. Because we are so used to acquiring new possessions we have come to accept planned obsolescence as a perfectly normal fact of life. The turnover of computers, cell phones, monitors and other high-tech toys is an almost yearly enterprise, yet it is very costly in almost every sense.

No part of our industrial process is immune to the rapid manufacture, dissemination and then perceived obsolescence and subsequent trashing of products. In many cases perfectly good working products are discarded because they no longer have the latest bells and whistles. No sooner is a product brought to market than it finds a saturation point, is upgraded and reintroduced as a new, improved product that pushes the old one into the dustbin. This cycle is repeated many times over for almost every product we have. It has created a massive mountain of refuse and in the process deprived our co-species of habitat to the point where many of them are either extinct or on the brink of extinction.

Consumerism and planned obsolescence are twin evils that now plague the globe. Our refuse is found in every part of the world and no area is spared. Thousands of kilometres out to sea we have massive floating slicks of plastic, oil, detritus and the bodies of the creatures unfortunate enough to come in contact with these toxic and dangerous floating dumps. There is plastic in the desert of Iran, Antarctica and the Himalayan mountains. Walk along any beach or coastal area in the Maritimes and you will find this evidence of our industry. Mountains of plastic and other refuse wash up on our shores, inexorably, day after day. To produce this garbage we have to do a number of things, all of them bad. We extract the hydrocarbon from the ground, which is becoming an increasingly energy intensive enterprise, which in itself increases climate change gases; we ship it to refineries, again at significant energy cost, refine and extract the materials that we want, usually burning off the rest, then ship the raw hydrocarbons to various manufacturing centres and again create the products that we want. When we ship oil, whether in tankers or through pipelines, we run the risk of accidents, environmental disasters, spills and leaks.

In our efforts to decrease waste we have adopted the three Rs: reduce, recycle and reuse. While laudable and by far a much better ethic compared to the rampant consumerism of the past half century in the West, they will not be more than a first step. Our ecological footprint needs to be reduced by at least a factor of ten in order to have a significant impact. That means that every person in the West has to reduce garbage, energy consumption and resources by 90 percent.

Our economy is based on consumption. It is no accident that more and more frequently people are referred to as consumers rather than citizens. Our cities are set up to deal with the concerns of businesses, which in turn are based on the economy of growth. We are bombarded with ads telling us that new is good and old is to be thrown out. Our transportation grids are laid out so that workers can travel to serve business. Just-in-time efficiency models mandate transportation of parts to the cheapest labour pools and then ship the consumables to massive big box stores for sale. Everything in our society is designed for consumption.

Fast Food

For a good example, let's look at the aptly-named fast food business. The way we eat has had an incredible morphology in the past half century. Back in the 1960s popular science articles used to speculate that our technological advances would provide people with so much leisure time that finding meaningful activities to fill out the week might be a problem. Service industries and repetitive, menial tasks would be done by robots. Every convenience would be at our fingertips and differences in income would be a thing of the past.

Today's world is almost diametrically opposed to this vision. We work longer hours, live in congested cities and in spite of the increased hours of work, individual incomes have fallen. In short, people are doing more for less. In the process of rushing to fill the business models of consumerism, there is less time for everything. Even getting to work is becoming more work as our cities expand. Our cars become our surrogate environments, where everything from conception to death is lived out. Even eating has been reduced to a business where time is the most important ingredient. Today a full 50 percent of all meals eaten in North America comes from fast food restaurants.

The irony is that fast food restaurant offerings are not good from just about every perspective. It's unhealthy to eat fast foods and it's unhealthy for the planet.

It would be easy to poke fun at the proliferation of American fast food restaurants, but we here in Canada, and especially the Maritimes, have one of the largest homegrown fast food chains in the world. In Canada, Tim Hortons is the largest fast food chain with twice as many restaurants as McDonald's, the largest fast food chain in the world. As of early 2008, Tim Hortons had 2,710 stores in Canada.

Some Fast (Down and Dirty Rough Stats) Food for Thought

No hard statistics are available for a Maritime breakdown, but assuming there is continuity in stats across Canada we can do a rough estimate. The Maritimes' 6 percent of the population means we probably also have 6 percent of the stores. To take my rough arithmetic even further, suppose that the stats for fast food consumption in Canada apply on average to the Maritimes. In 2005 one-quarter of Canadians ate at least one meal at a fast food outlet. That gives us 500,000 meals per day. Also assuming that each meal produced 100 grams of waste, that would be 100 x 500,000 = 50,000,000 grams = 50,000 kilograms = 50 metric tonnes of waste (most of it paper) each and every day. That would equal 18,250 tonnes of paper each year.

Now let's break down that waste. Assuming that a pulp log weighs 500 kilograms and comes from one tree, that would mean that about 36,000 trees would need to be felled to provide the paper for fast food meals in the Maritimes. Now assuming we get about 1,000 of these trees per hectare, that would mean each year we cut down 36 hectares of trees just for the waste on fast food. Now most of this either lies in landfills, is thrown into the environment or burned. If it winds up being burned it adds immediately to CO_2. Assuming that half of it is burned, 9,000 tonnes of CO_2 is added to the air.

And there is more.

During its life, each year that tree would take about 20 kilograms of carbon out of the ecosystem. For 36,000 trees that comes to 720,000 kilograms or 720 tonnes. Add this to the burned waste and the deficit in terms of CO_2 is almost 10,000 tonnes, just for paper to wrap food and beverages in the Maritimes.

But we aren't finished yet. To get the tree into paper we have to cut it, truck it and pulp it, which all add to the energy waste and CO_2 waste. The trucks have to be manufactured and shipped and so on. It's a cycle that doesn't end! Let's assume then that it has to get to market, is itself wrapped before it is used and we get a horrible waste just for the convenience of a snack. Just some fast food for thought.

Much of the product that we consume in fast food stores is not prepared within the store, but rather shipped from centralized locations, some thousands of kilometres away. Hamburgers and hot dogs are made from meat from animals that are grown all over the world and shipped to depots after they have been processed. It is not unusual for a Maritimer to eat a hamburger or sandwich made of meat from beef/pork/chicken raised in Argentina, Hawaii and/or Alberta, processed in Toronto, frozen and flown to the Moncton or Summerside outlet to be cooked and prepared and packaged for local consumption.

More Food for Thought

The Maritimes have a relatively short growing season to produce the food we need to eat and to feed the animals we eventually consume. We have about two million mouths to feed in the Maritimes and assuming that we eat roughly 2,500 calories per day per person that gives us about five billion calories per day. Assuming that a pound of fat is equal to 3,500 calories, we need 680,000 kilograms of fat equivalent food to sustain us each and every day in the Maritimes. In the course of a year we would need 1.5 million animals at approximately 165 kilograms each to sustain the entire Maritime population for a year. A 700-kilogram steer would sustain about four Maritimers but take two years to grow, so we can assume one steer for every two Maritimers. So if we got all our nutrition from beef we would need roughly one million steers to sustain us for a year. One steer would take the resources of 45 hectares, giving us 2.4 steers per square kilometre. One million steers would require approximately 480,000 square kilometres to grow, if we fed them only from local land. The total area of the Maritimes is under 140,000 square kilometres, less than a third of the land required to feed us if we were to subsist on beef fed off the land.

This is only an illustration to show how much our population consumes. In actual fact, beef makes up a small percentage of the total caloric requirements and there are efficiencies realized by consuming plants, such as grain, potatoes, fruits and vegetables. The point is that not all of the land in the Maritimes can be or should be used to feed us. It is a simple and oversimplified illustration to show that even though our population is small compared to many other areas of the world, it is not when compared to the capacity to sustain us.

Agribusiness

Farming, like so many things today, has become industrialized and most of our food is now grown on a vast scale, according to business. Agriculture has become agribusiness. In the opinion of many writers and anthropologists, agriculture is the single most important invention of the human species and is what has enabled us to create civilization. Jared Diamond lays out a wonderful treatise for the importance of agriculture in both *Guns, Germs and Steel: The Fates of Societies* and *Collapse: How Societies Choose to Fail or Succeed*. Without agriculture, the growing of the handful of plant and animal species for food that sustain us, our civilization would not have happened.

Even though agribusiness has been able to provide food efficiently and in the quantities we need, the costs to the environment have been immense. The reduced forest cover, ecological habitat decline and the introduction of domestic species on such a vast scale has had an unprecedented effect. We have been able to feed ourselves, but the infrastructure of land, air and water has been seriously undermined. In addition, because of genetic modification, we rely on very few plant and animal species for food at the expense of our natural surroundings. This loss of crop, seed and animal diversification represents a serious threat to global ecosystem health.

Globally, there are about 1.3 billion cattle, by far dwarfing any number of non-domestic animals on Earth. That is one cow for every five people. The population of cattle is only possible through modern agribusiness methods where cattle feed comes from almost any source of organic protein, including other cattle. The methane released by all these cattle is substantial and a contributing factor to global warming, accounting for about one-third of the people-made methane that finds its way into the atmosphere.

PEI Farming Stats (from Statistics Canada): Prince Edward Island, known as the Million Acre Farm, has a total land area of only 5,684 square kilometres. The total farming area is about 2,615 square kilometres, making almost 50 percent of the island under agricultural use. Roads, clearings and urban areas take up another 35 percent of the total, leaving a paltry 15 percent of the total land undeveloped. In 2001 PEI had 1,845 farms, but by 2006 it was down to 1,700.

In spite of the obvious savings in raising our own supply of meat locally, we still stock our supermarket shelves with imported meat. A worst case scenario shows it costs eight kilograms of carbon dioxide emissions for each kilogram of lamb shipped from New Zealand to the Maritimes. Compare that to just seven grams of CO_2 for locally grown lamb per kilogram. It's a scale of environmental efficiency of over 100,000 percent or 1,000 times more environmentally efficient, from a CO_2 perspective, to grow locally!

Nova Scotia Farming Overview from Statistics Canada: In the 1920s and 1930s Nova Scotia was the world's largest producer of apples. After 20 years of economic stability, the province lost its European market with the onset of World War II. This marked the decline of the agricultural sector in Nova Scotia. Though diminished, it continues to be important because of its impact on the provincial and local economies. During the late 1950s and 1960s the government encouraged farmers to take on low-cost credit assistance from the Farm Credit Corporation to increase the size of their farms and to make them more technologically advanced.

In the 1996 census, Statistics Canada determined there were 4,453 farms in Nova Scotia. In 2001, the total number of farms dropped to 3,923 and further declined to 2,795 by 2006. Nova Scotia has fewer agricultural operations and produces less farm revenue than some counties in Ontario.

Nova Scotia's total area used for farming purposes is roughly 4,000 square kilometres or 7.5 percent of its total area.

In total, there are about 110,000 cattle in the Maritimes, about 150,000 sheep and hogs and almost one million chickens, which provide about one-quarter of all the meat consumed in the Maritimes. As a result, most of the meat consumed comes from outside of the three provinces. But what is grown is for the most part consumed within local markets. It stays close to local and regional markets with much of it winding up in local stores and restaurants. This transportation energy saving helps offset the other detriments on meat versus plant consumption.

Agriculture has become a business and like any business it is concerned with maximizing profits. Consequently, the most efficient farming practices are those that delete competition from other plants and implement uni/monocultures. This lowers the biodiversity and creates a loss of habitat. This in turn means lower absorption of climate change gases because of reduced forest and fallow lands.

> New Brunswick Farming Stats from Statistics Canada: New Brunswick has less land under farming than either Nova Scotia or PEI. Most of this has to do with the importance of the lumber industry to the economy and to the harsher climate, which makes the growing of crops for human and animal feed less efficient and more expensive. The total area under cultivation is just over 1,300 square kilometres, which is about 2 percent of the total land area. In 2001 there were 3,034 farms; by 2006 the number had declined to 2,776.

To sustain the yields, monocultures also use pesticides and fertilizers. The water runoff from pesticide-laden fields creates toxic rivers and lakes, which in turn has an added deleterious effect on natural ecosystems. And with the climate we have in the Maritimes, cleared land devoid of trees for agriculture is only productive for a short part of each year.

While meat has obvious disadvantages from an ecological standpoint – methane emissions, effluent, inefficient use of food-stuffs, displaced indigenous animals, and loss of habitat – plants from current agribusiness methods also have negative impacts. Rice paddies emit a substantial proportion of the total anthropogenic methane emitted into the atmosphere. Monocultures also displace indigenous plant species and can contribute to wide-scale soil loss.

In general, plants provide a more ecologically friendly source of food than do animals and there are methods of cultivation that can make the impact surprisingly small. In the Maritimes it is very difficult to sidestep the issue of the short growing season. It is a fact of life that many food plants cannot be grown in the Maritimes. But there are ways to use technology to deal with this. One method that has found some good results is to use greenhouses. Heating greenhouses with non-fossil fuels extends the growing season to make year-round cultivation possible. In addition, greenhouses are a closed environment, which means that pests, such as competing plants and insects, can be better controlled, often almost totally without the use of chemical pesticides. And finally greenhouses use area far more efficiently because they can grow plants year-round, increasing productivity and can even be stacked, if proper energy efficient heat and light can be procured.

Paper and Plastic

Paper or plastic? Which is better environmentally? Both paper and plastic when put into landfills will remain there for hundreds of years. If burned, instead of being buried, both paper and plastic not only release global warming gases into the atmosphere but also a myriad of toxic gases including furans and dioxins, which are among the most carcinogenic substances known.

Homemade Paper and Plastic Mountains: The average Maritime family throws out 20 kilograms of paper and plastic each week. With roughly 500,000 families that makes for 50 million kilograms of paper and plastic each week and a total of just under 20 billion kilograms or 20 million tonnes each year.

To produce half a kilogram of plastic, one litre of oil or half a kilogram of coal must be extracted from the ground, shipped, processed, manufactured and shipped again to the sales outlet. In addition to the processing, we need machinery to mine it, which is invariably run on diesel. The rippling effect is difficult to stop, because the machinery on which we depend to create the plastic has to be itself manufactured from the raw materials. It's an almost endless cycle.

In short, that half a kilo or one pound of plastic is in effect worth its weight in CO_2 emissions to produce. In the Maritimes all the raw hydrocarbon plastic is shipped long distances, which also requires fuel and machinery. We do have oil refineries, where the crude is fractionated – that is, broken down through complex heating and cooling processes – but once that happens, we again ship the material around the world for additional processing and distribute the raw plastics back into our markets.

If this seems like a lot of shipping, it is. By the time the completed plastic product winds up in the grocery store or in any other store for that matter, the plastic is a seasoned world traveller with an almost unbelievable carbon footprint.

When plastic finally finds its way into the mountainous Maritime landfills, it is likely to outlast anything else that we throw away and will continue to leach chlorine and fluorine compounds and CO_2 into the environment for years to come. That plastic throwaway wrap, while very cheaply manufactured, is actually very expensive and a large part of our CO_2 footprint.

Paper's footprint is different, but also significant. When comparing plastic to paper it's very difficult to determine which has a more deleterious effect on the environment and the atmosphere. Ultimately, all paper comes from trees and in the Maritimes, especially New Brunswick, trees and forestry are big, big business. Trees are also a major consumer of CO_2. When we cut them down for processing into paper products we take a powerful CO_2 inhibitor out of the environmental mix and add the CO_2 of processing into the atmosphere for a double environmental whammy. The processing of most paper products uses a host of noxious chemicals that have detrimental effects on both the water and the air.

In the end, it is hard to say whether paper is more or less friendly to the environment than plastic-related products. It depends on the degree of processing, shipping and, of course, chemical additives.

Habitat

How we live is as important as where we live. The type of home, how it is designed, how energy efficient, its size, location within the community, access to rapid transportation, material used and energy supply are all important considerations in how and where we live.

New designs as well as heating and cooling systems have revolutionized modern construction methods. R-2000 homes, even ten years ago, used to be an anomaly. Now they are commonplace. We are just beginning to learn about better ways to live. Homes require heating, cooling, space, materials, renovations, electricity, communications and a myriad of devices that absorb ever increasing amounts of energy to run, replace and retire. Add to that the location of the home and how close it is to amenities such as public transit, shops, work and schools and you get some idea of how energy intensive our homes are today.

The urban sprawl brought on by our suburban culture is at the core of the transportation/home/work conundrum. In Canada, the sprawls from our largest centres (Toronto, Montreal, Calgary and Vancouver) have eaten up vast amounts of fallow and agricultural land and contributed to greenhouse gas emissions in two ways. The construction of a home uses up raw materials and land. It also deletes trees and other plants from the ecosystem that mitigate increases in gases such as CO_2.

In the past 50 years, specifically because of the car, we have created a unique and surprisingly destructive type of habitat – the suburb.

The suburbs, in which one-fifth of all North Americans live, were invented in New York in 1947. Levittown was built on what used to be potato farms in an area known as Island Trees. On May 7, 1947, Levitt and Sons announced their plan to build 2,000 mass-produced rental homes for veterans. Two days later, the *New York Herald Tribune* reported that 1,000 of the 2,000 proposed homes had already been rented. Levittown, as the new development would eventually be named, was off to a booming start. The rest is history. Virtually every other city in North America picked on the "bedroom community" style development.

To build their homes cheaper and faster, Levitt and Sons wanted to eliminate basements and build on concrete slabs instead, as they had in Norfolk, Virginia. This practice was prohibited in the Town of Hempstead but, because the need for housing was so urgent, the town modified their building code to allow the Levitts to proceed.

Levitt and Sons used many of the building methods they had used over the years in previous developments, but reorganized these methods for even better efficiency and cost savings. All the lumber was precut and shipped from a lumber yard they owned in Blue Lake, California, where they erected a nail factory as well. An abandoned rail line was reopened to bring construction materials to Island Trees. To keep costs down, although it met with heavy opposition, non-union contractors were used. The production line technique used to build this new development was so successful that by July 1948, the Levitts were turning out 30 houses a day.

It is not uncommon for commuters in cities, in the suburbs and beyond to spend an hour and a half travelling each way to work and home every day, much of that time stalled in gridlock.

The Maritimes' largest city is Halifax and though its traffic problems pale beside those of Toronto, it is evident that it too suffers from a significant suburban sprawl. It appears that we have not learned from the plight of the many urban predecessors in North America. We continue to build suburbs that are primarily designed for the automobile.

Most of the new developments in our cities are dominated by suburban homes. In addition to requiring more energy to sustain, heat and cool, they also use up more resources per home. In western Europe, where space and energy are at a premium, most cities are now building vertically and building homes that are smaller and less based on car transportation. Monster homes and suburban sprawl are being countered with city core renovation and revitalization.

The Raw Wood Facts: 99 percent of the wood harvested in the Maritimes comes from clearcut methods, what environmentalists believe is the worst and most habitat-destructive method of harvesting wood.

Much of the raw wood for home construction is milled and processed locally, but a substantial proportion of wood requires finishing to create wood products and is shipped overseas, processed and shipped back to the Maritimes for consumption. This creates a significant and easily rectified CO_2 cost to a product that is grown and harvested locally.

Over three-quarters of the wood harvested in the Maritimes is shipped to the United States. Of the remaining 25 percent, more than half is shipped overseas and almost all the rest is used in local building and for heat. Almost all the processed furniture and wood products we buy in our stores, even though it may originally come from the Maritimes, is processed abroad and shipped back for us to consume.

Apartment buildings, condominiums and cluster developments that utilize as small a physical space as possible are now becoming more attractive because of reduced costs and energy savings. Apartments are cheaper to heat and cool per unit home, because fewer walls are exposed to energy losses to the outside. As the core regions of cities become more sought after, this type of dwelling is becoming more popular. Increased population densities have the added benefit of making it cost efficient and expedient to have core services, like health care, shopping and public transit. It also makes people less dependent on automobiles.

For those who still want independent single dwelling homes, innovations in home design and construction are growing faster than ever. New homes incorporate computer technology to meet increased energy efficiency. Individual rooms can be heated and cooled as needed, rather than being regulated by a central heating system that heats and cools the house en masse.

Wood still remains the most popular building material for a variety of reasons. It is simple to use, has many applications, is lightweight, strong, a renewable material, and degrades well into the environment after its usefulness has expired.

It takes 30 to 40 years for trees to grow to harvestable size (given the location) and in that time a tree can absorb ten tonnes of CO_2 – or the amount of CO_2 produced by an average passenger car in four years.

Other Building Materials and Methods

Concrete is a very popular construction material, and in the Maritimes almost every house, apartment building and commercial site uses amazing amounts of concrete. What most don't realize is that production of the Portland cement in concrete creates vast amounts of CO_2.

Making Portland cement causes environmental impacts at all stages of the process. These include emissions of airborne pollution in the form of dust and gases, when operating machinery and during blasting in quarries, consumption of large quantities of fuel during manufacture, release of CO_2 from the raw materials during manufacture, and damage to the countryside from quarrying.

The CO_2 associated with Portland cement manufacture falls into three categories:

* CO_2 derived from decarbonation of limestone. About half a kilogram of CO_2 is produced for every kilogram of cement through this process.

* CO_2 from kiln fuel combustion. About half a kilogram of CO_2 per kilogram of cement is produced from this method.

* CO_2 produced by vehicles in cement plants and distribution. This source is by far the smallest, yet not insignificant when considering the amount of cement used every day, about 0.1 kilogram per kilo of cement.

In total, roughly one kilogram of CO_2 is produced for every kilogram of cement.

Maritime Cement Estimates: About one kilogram of CO_2 is produced for every kilogram of cement. If we assume the average home uses ten tonnes of cement in its construction and that 30,000 new homes are built annually in the Maritimes, that gives us a production of 300,000 tonnes of CO_2 released in the cement alone each year. Note that these stats do not reflect commercial construction, highways or other concrete infrastructures.

The way to mitigate CO_2 costs for concrete is to use less of it. Concrete is a very valuable building material, necessary for any construction. However, by using granite and other durable and inert rocks for the foundations of our smaller homes we can cut down on the amount of cement used and still maintain the structural integrity of our homes. Larger buildings such as apartments and high-rises have no suitable replacement, so cement and concrete will continue to be the only material that allows for these buildings to be constructed.

In Europe, experimental designs are showing that homes can reduce their CO_2 footprint by building dwellings with much of the living space underground or homes that support a roof with soil on which plants can be grown. Whether these types of homes are viable in the Maritimes remains to be seen, but it is worth the research and effort to see if these homes can reduce energy consumption.

BioEnergy

Over the past couple of years, we have been hearing more about biofuels and how they will be the panacea for our CO_2 production woes. The short answer to this is that everything and anything that burns, whether it is alcohol, gasoline, diesel, cooking fat or kerosene, produces CO_2. The bottom line is we can have a much bigger impact on the environment and the production of CO_2 by slowing down our vehicles. In the Maritimes, if we slowed down and saved the 50 percent of the CO_2 emissions, that would mean a very conservative saving of 25,000 tonnes of CO_2 per week, which translates to a whopping 12.5 million tonnes of CO_2 per year.

At best, the introduction of alcohol and other hybrid biofuels would decrease CO_2 emissions by as little as 5 percent or even less, once all the environmental impacts have been taken into account. It would also increase the land used for the growing of biofuels, taking it out of the natural, fallow ecosystem. It would increase the use of pesticides, which presents more of an energy deficit as well as the inevitable toxic runoff. Finally, it has the effect of making people feel they are being ecologically responsible, when in fact they are not.

Hydrogen

Hydrogen as a fuel has the ability, when burned, to produce zero CO_2 emissions. All that the burning of hydrogen produces is water and heat. It is a wonderful fuel, just for that reason alone. So why haven't we jumped on the hydrogen bandwagon and converted every gas station, truck and automobile to use hydrogen? The answer is in the chemistry of hydrogen. What makes it a great fuel is also what makes it very hard and expensive to produce, store and use as such.

Hydrogen makes an excellent chemical fuel because it has only one proton in its nucleus and one electron. The key to its usefulness as a fuel substitute is that single electron. Hydrogen is used to operate many rockets and a portion of the space shuttle, so you can get an idea of its power.

When oxygen bonds with hydrogen, or burns, it gives off a huge amount of energy. Bring oxygen and hydrogen together and with even the slightest spark you can have an immediate conflagration. The Hindenberg zeppelin is a perfect example of what happens. On May 6, 1937, it caught fire while docking at Lakehurst Naval Air Station in New Jersey, burning up in 37 seconds, killing 13 of the 36 passengers and 22 of the 61 crew.

The great news is as this release of energy happens and the hydrogen burns with the oxygen, all you get is water, pure water, and heat. Nothing else.

The bad news is because we have so much free oxygen on Earth, any hydrogen we have is pretty much all gobbled up by the oxygen and exists as water already. There is a huge amount of hydrogen tied up in water. Two hydrogen atoms for every molecule of water. That's why it is called H_2O.

More bad news. Trying to get at that hydrogen so we can use it as fuel requires an energy source to break it away from the oxygen. A lot of energy. The process of splitting water into oxygen and hydrogen is electrohydrolysis. So we wind up having to pay an energy cost to get energy. So what do we do? We can't burn coal to provide the electricity to break the bonds in water, because that is what we are trying to stop. The reason we are considering hydrogen as a fuel is because it is powerful, portable and non-polluting ... almost three Ps.

So engineers and scientists think it is worthwhile to consider hydrogen as a fuel source to power our travel needs, because that is what we are looking for – something powerful, portable and non-polluting. In gasoline and other liquid fossils fuels we have the powerful and portable part pretty much solved. It's in the non-polluting area that we fall down. And because the internal combustion engine has caught on in such a big way we have a CO_2 problem. If we didn't want or need to travel so much then CO_2 from travel wouldn't be so much of an issue. But we do and it is, so we have to reconsider.

Hydrogen is not only found in water. It is also in methane – CH_4 – and all the other hydrocarbons, including gasoline. Anytime we burn hydrocarbon fuels a portion of the emissions is water, including carbon dioxide. The problem is that because carbon is found in all these fossil fuels, carbon dioxide finds its way into the equation. Hydrogen, on the other hand, only produces heat and water and zero carbon dioxide.

Engineers have now created a number of other energy sources that are becoming viable and do not involve fossil fuels, which is good as far as the non-polluting aspect, but are not very powerful or portable. So they have proposed solutions that range from things like solar energy, to tidal energy to wind power to create the energy necessary to fractionate water.

> Maritime Tide Fact: We, in the Maritimes, have the highest tides in the world, which means we have an enormous potential energy source that is non-polluting and, just as good, reliable. The great thing about tides is that they come and go twice every day, and in the Bay of Fundy the water is equivalent to dozens of Niagaras. By harnessing the tides we would have a peerless, renewable and virtually endless source of energy – all because we have a moon.

In terms of energy, initial estimates show tidal power in the Maritimes to be better than solar and wind for a variety of reasons. Solar power requires high technology and exotic materials, many of them highly toxic when they get into the environment, not to mention the fact that sunshine is often in short supply. Solar panels also have a limited lifetime. Wind also suffers from reliability, though not so much in the Maritimes as other places, but also requires huge turbines that make noise, are a threat to birds, are not all that pretty to look at and break down.

Using tides as an energy source taps into hydroelectric power, which has a very tried and true technology used around the world. In fact, Canada is a world leader in the generation of electricity from flowing water. Adapting hydro technology to tidal power to generate electricity would appear to be the shortest and most efficient energy route to creating clean electricity for consumption and for making hydrogen. However, there is another wrinkle in the hydrogen equation. It's called storage.

Hydrogen is portable – only just. What makes gasoline so great as a fuel is that while it is volatile, it is also easily stored and easy to carry around without the burden of high technology or complicated, costly systems. Not so for hydrogen. Hydrogen is very light and a gas at room temperatures. That means you don't get a lot of the stuff into a container without bumping into a number of technical issues.

You have to compress hydrogen to enormous pressures. In addition, while very powerful as a fuel, it has about four times the energy per weight compared to gasoline. That means you have to compress hydrogen even more. And compression takes energy and the storage tanks get heavier and heavier the higher the compression.

Hydrogen can be liquified, which gives it a higher volumetric energy density. However, liquid hydrogen is cryogenic so it is only a liquid at very, very cold temperatures and boils around 20.268 Kelvin (–252.882°C or -423.188°F). This also takes a lot of energy and again lowers the efficiency of hydrogen as a fuel. To hold liquid hydrogen, tanks have to be very well insulated to prevent boil off. Then there is the problem of ice, which may form around the tank and help corrode it further if the insulation fails. Insulation for liquid hydrogen tanks is usually expensive and delicate.

As it stands, the storage and containment of hydrogen so that it can be used efficiently for travel is the major stumbling block for creating a hydrogen economy.

Nuclear Power

The spectacular failures of Chernobyl and Three Mile Island, along with the documented medical horrors of Nagasaki and Hiroshima, have tainted public attitudes to nuclear power. That is not to say that nuclear power cannot be considered, but if we consider it for use, it must be used very, very cautiously and the true costs of its use worked into the energy equation. It is still questionable whether we as a society have the discipline to mitigate the very substantial dangers that nuclear power presents.

Nuclear power has the distinct benefit of offering zero emissions of climate change gases. When compared to coal-fired plants in terms of GHG emissions it's no contest. It can generate vast amounts of electricity and has in many countries been a safe and viable power generation alternative. The fear and trepidation of nuclear power comes from the fact that the fissile material used to create the core of the reactor remains radioactive for thousands of years. No one has yet designed a complete cradle-to-grave foolproof nuclear reactor. Gamma radiation is very dangerous and there are no safe levels.

In terms of reliability, the latest generation of nuclear reactors, the third generation, offers fail-safe systems many times higher than those of reactors built even 20 years ago.

Because nuclear power plants do not generate any greenhouse gases during the generation of electricity, it is attractive to at least consider them as a power generating option. But the overwhelming issue remains the spectre of radioactivity from design and mechanical failure, spent fuel and the relatively new threat of terrorism. Does that make them a viable alternative? It's a complicated question and one that has no clear-cut answers. It's also one that has become highly charged and polarized. Those who like them, like them a lot and those who dislike them, dislike them a lot. There does not seem to be any middle ground.

Coal-fired plants release massive amounts of climate change gases and other pollutants that range from mercury to sulphur dioxide into the air. The number of deaths and injuries, including birth defects and environmental degradation, that can be attributed to these plants is in the hundreds of thousands each year. In addition, once the pollutants reach the environment there is no way to track them, let alone retrieve them for safe disposition. As an example, the summer heat wave of 2003 that struck Europe killed more than 14,000 in Paris alone. Climatologists attribute the extreme summer heat to the changes in the climate brought about by the burning of fossil fuels.

On the other hand, nuclear radiation is easy to track even in the tiniest amounts. If any radioactive materials are left in the environment they can be tracked with even the simplest technology. Geiger counters, which have been around for almost a century, are efficient, cheap and reliable.

The real problem is what to do with the waste of a nuclear power plant. Everything that the radioactive byproduct comes in contact with becomes radioactive. Once the enriched uranium has been spent and is of no further use in the reactor core, it has to be replaced with new fuel. Unfortunately, the spent fuel is still incredibly radioactive and will remain so for a very, very long time.

Radiation also has the disadvantage of changing the chemistry of its surroundings so that containers designed to hold radioactive materials safely in isolation for centuries, in fact, break down in a matter of years.

If nuclear power is to be considered a viable short-term power source we have to solve the problem of what to do with the wastes. If, over the next decade, the containment issues plaguing the nuclear industry are addressed, then nuclear power will be able to off-load the energy burden from fossil fuels and in the short term ameliorate the obvious energy issues.

New Brunswick Nuclear Fact: New Brunswick has the only nuclear power plant in the Maritimes. NB Power Nuclear is responsible for operating the Point Lepreau Generating Station. The 635-megawatt unit, commissioned in 1983, was the first CANDU-6 to begin commercial operation. The station has exceeded one million person-hours without a lost-time accident on three occasions.

Point Lepreau has been a reliable generator during its 23 years of operation – its in-service capacity factor is approximately 83 percent, slightly above design performance expectations. The facility accounts for up to 30 percent of in-province generation.

Lepreau also requires expensive and extensive maintenance. It is now closed for 18 months (March 2008 to September 2009) for refurbishment, which includes replacing all the 380 fuel channels, calandria tubes and feeder pipes as well as other maintenance. It is the first CANDU-6 reactor to have this type of work done.

5

Acting –
Private, Government and Individual

It's Never too Late ... Is it?

How much time do we have to solve the problem and when is it too late to act? When do our actions become just rearranging the deck chairs on the *Titanic*?

The long and the short of it is, we have to educate ourselves so we can understand what will work, what is obfuscation, what has hidden agendas and what can really be achieved. We even have to address what we once thought were inalienable rights, like the right to procreate without any concern for the population or the right to live anywhere and anyhow we want, because we have the money or the ability to introduce new products and create planned obsolescence. Monster homes, SUVs, speeding, consumption, growth, NIMBY (not in my backyard), and a host of other habits that add to climate change and environmental degradation have yet to become a day-to-day public priority.

We need to see the true cost of everything, from food and how far it has been transported to get to the dinner table, to processing of materials overseas because much lower labour costs offset the travel expenses, to overpackaging. It's all about the facts and being able to make decisions based on what is the lowest environmental cost overall. In order to do that each of us has to understand that climate change is not some plot that has been cooked up by a bunch of "tree huggers." We have to learn that understanding comes from the facts, the studies and digging a bit deeper than the six o'clock television news.

Much of the information we rely on, especially television news, is skewed or even scientifically inaccurate. In-depth reporting just does not happen, especially in the sciences because most reporters have no understanding of science or scientific method. We need to get off the junk science, spectacle-laden reporting of science that masquerades as fact, and begin to understand the problem by using our most powerful tool, education.

Is it too late? That is a good and important question.

Costs and Jobs

It is a popular perception in Canada that somebody else has to make the changes, because we have too small an effect to make a difference. Listening to the politicians and business leaders we get the perspective that China and India or the United States are the problem, that they have the populations and the industries that create the bulk of climate change.

Another argument says we will damage our economy to the point that we will never recover and the jobs that sustain our society, way of life and innovation will disappear.

If you buy this type of argument, you have a perfect recipe for doing nothing.

If we begin research at home, begin the engineering, funding, support, financial incentives and create technologies to slow the advance of climate change, it becomes an exportable commodity, a source of employment and revenue and stability.

Now is the time to look at the hydrogen economy, tidal power projects, wind power, wave power, sail innovation, nuclear options and greenhouse agriculture. We have a highly educated workforce, world-ranked educational institutions, a stable government system and the opportunity to become global leaders in Green Technology that, once created, can be exported worldwide.

The coming climate change, rather than being a damper on the Maritime economy, could provide an enormous boost to employment. On the other hand, if we choose to wait, climate change will continue to happen anyway and other countries will take advantage of the opportunities.

New Planning

As the climate changes the main challenge will be to adapt. Adapting requires us to have some idea of where the changes are taking us, how far and how intense these changes will be. Once we understand that, we can begin to plan what will happen as temperatures climb, precipitation amounts increase, storm frequency and intensity increase. But it is not just the weather and the climate that will be altered. In response to climate change the biosphere will also adjust. These changes are potentially huge. An invasion of new plants, animals and even pathogens can be expected as well as the attendant extinctions and out-migrations of what are today common species.

Disaster planning is only part of the equation. What follows is a short list of some of the issues we will have to plan to contend with.

Less is More

An immediate concern is our economy and its role in climate change. Our current economic models are all based on ever increasing consumption and growth. This growth has led to a dramatic increase of life expectancy, standard of living and consumption, but at a huge cost to the environment. It has been a trade-off between our prosperity and standard of living versus the health of the environment. Until 50 years ago the trade-off still left lots of unspoiled wilderness. Over the past 50 years we have overwhelmed the Earth's ability to absorb and recover from our onslaught.

We must re-examine the growth mandate. We need new economic models that will allow us to function and be prosperous without the need to have constant growth in order to avoid economic disaster.

Business has traditionally operated without concern for the environment. The environment is considered a consumable resource and only has value as raw material for the economy. A tree's only worth is through the products we make, such as furniture or paper. It has no value in business esthetically as habitat or air exchanger.

Our next step must be to re-examine our consumptive models and all the impacts of our industry, including and especially the environmental. A tree has worth outside business.

Education and Communication

These twins go hand in hand. Obfuscation and rhetoric is only possible if the public remains uneducated. In order to be educated we have to maintain our research facilities and our data collection. The Maritimes are blessed with world-class educational institutions and per capita we have the greatest number of post-secondary facilities in Canada.

For this information and understanding to become part of common knowledge, we have to make sure it is communicated. And in that area we have sadly fallen behind. Journalists, storytellers and the media in general are not science oriented and have very little understanding of the sciences or scientific method and how to differentiate between rhetoric and the hard facts. Our media, print, Internet, TV and radio have to make efforts to upgrade their understanding of the issues, the science behind the issues and resist the urge to glorify and hyperbolize. Controversy for controversy's sake ultimately serves no one. Chasing ambulances and the ethic of "if it bleeds it leads" (a newsroom term based on rating which stories are most important) need to be excoriated from the journalist's old stand-bys. Peer review is a process, not an end. Scientists are the most conservative segment of society because their studies are always critically examined, criticized and critiqued by other scientists. Flaws are analyzed and addressed.

In the same way, studies and interpretations and the climate and weather are constantly pitting one stream of thought and conjecture against another. Scientists don't so much line up on one side or the other on the issue of human-induced climate change, but rather interpret the studies and information to come up with the most likely conclusions. In covering the stories where one stream of scientific thought supersedes another, it is journalists who make the controversy in order to give the story a "human" element.

What Government Can Do

How we behave determines how our society functions. All levels of government will have to create bodies whose purpose will be to understand the science behind climate change and communicate that to their prospective levels of government. For this to happen we need a consensus, an agreement, not only between various Canadian governments but internationally. We will need experts in law and the environment, people who are literate in what works, what doesn't and how to implement laws and guidelines that are not only effective but palatable. And when draconian action must be taken, we must know how to communicate the necessity of the laws to the public.

> None of the provincial governments in Canada has a science advisor whose sole purpose is to interpret and advise the premier and cabinet on the advances and changes in science. The Maritimes would benefit greatly from a specialist in science and the environment to advise and make recommendations to the premiers and cabinets.

We need to consider things like a consumption law. If the world only had a population of 250 million people, everyone could drive whatever they wanted to drive, fly where they wanted and live in vast energy-consuming homes. But with a population 25 times that and growing we have pushed the environment to its limits. Individuals have to become aware of the issues and expect the same from their elected officials.

The Role of Industry

Though many industries are becoming "greener" by building more efficient plants, reusing materials and consuming less energy, this is not nearly enough to make a real difference to human-induced climate change. Our industry serves a consumer society and that is the real issue we have to tackle. It's not enough to make the consumer goods we purchase more energy efficient or the plants in which they are manufactured more environmentally friendly. The fact that we consume so much is what we need to address. Making a plant more efficient only addresses a small part of the environmental CO_2 problem.

A lot of print and paper has been wasted extolling the virtues of making the automobile more energy efficient. There are hybrid cars, hydrogen plans, electric cars, smaller cars and an array of projects designed to make the automobile two or three times more energy efficient. But a broader examination of the problem will show that this approach, which is an industrial approach and will keep the plants humming, just allows us to ease our consciences and does little to ease the climate change gas output of humanity.

The truth is that we have to re-examine the automobile industry and decide what we need to do to wean ourselves off the car. There are hundreds of millions of cars on the road and the number is climbing every day as one new car is manufactured every second.

And the automobile industry is just one example. Watches, handbags, computers, cell phones, appliances, homes and the list goes on and on and are all supported by our industrial base.

The consumption of manufactured products is what sustains our consumer society. We have equated a good life with our acquisitions and have allowed industry to create whatever it wants as long as there is a market for the product. If we have to re-examine the role of consumption, and all indications are that we do, then we also have to re-evaluate our industry and what we acquire, from cradle to grave.

Industry is adept at creating buzz and stimulating desires through advertising and marketing. Industry wants us to equate the good life with monetary wealth and possessions. Shopping has become an entertainment pastime where we browse stores to keep the consumer juggernaut rolling.

This is the major issue of the West and of the developing societies of China, India, Indonesia, Brazil and Russia. No matter how we look at downsizing the energy use of our manufacturing plants, by continuing to ignore consumption, planned obsolescence and industry, we will doom our efforts to wrestle climate change to the ground.

The Cost of Doing Nothing

It has been said that changing our ways in the face of climate change is too expensive, that we will collapse the economy if we address the concerns that have become increasingly obvious. The obvious retort is that the cost of doing nothing far outweighs doing something by such a great margin that we would have to be the most short-sighted creatures not to try to address climate change issues.

This all comes down to science and what I consider to be the most incredible invention ever, scientific method. It's really the simplest, most wonderful and most effective tool we have ever had, one that almost anyone can learn and benefit from.

Collect all the information, no matter how obscure and off the wall. Do not get trapped into editing the raw data, excluding information because of a bias or that it might invalidate the original hypothesis. Then apply the data to existing theory and see if it fits. That is where the hard work comes in. No theory is ever perfect nor does it explain everything all the time. All theories have a lifetime, before new information and facts modify or even completely replace them.

It's that way with the theories about human-induced climate change. Some scientists, even 100 years ago, thought that climate change was something we had to deal with along with our exponential increase in human population. The Club of Rome, a nonprofit global think tank, was predicting in the late 1960s that a catastrophic disaster would befall humankind by 2000 as resources ran out, food shortages occurred and environmental degradation took its toll. That obviously did not happen. It wasn't that the Club of Rome was out to lunch or a bunch of lunatics bent on catastrophizing.

What the Club of Rome was warning about is exactly what we are now concerned with. Technological advances were able to forestall the disasters they had predicted. Agribusiness, fertilizers, medicine and new advanced resource technologies all conspired to keep our burgeoning population fed, extend lifetimes and power our society. At the time of publication, the Club of Rome was basing its predictions on the best available information. The fact that disaster didn't happen does not invalidate the conjecture of the Club of Rome. Just like new unexpected technologies come to our rescue and force us to re-evaluate our theories, so too do new threats. CFCs (chloroflurocarbons), acid rain and ozone holes were ready to spring when the Club of Rome made its environmental predictions.

Each year the Ecology Action Centre in Halifax issues an overall environmental report card on the actions of the Maritime Provinces. In the decade or so that reports have been issued, all three provincial governments have fared poorly. In the past few years, the media have highlighted these reports and the poor performances of the Maritimes in making reductions in greenhouse gases. As a result, the governments have been forced to respond, as the public has become aware of how little is being done to address our obvious shortcomings.

Because of their work, the Club of Rome raised our environmental consciousness and made us aware that we were approaching a threshold, a tipping point. The fact that it is coming a bit later rather than sooner is something we should be very grateful for, because time is our most precious commodity.

If we rely on the hope that our amazing technology will bail us out of this predicament, then we are gambling with our and the planet's future. It may well be that an incredible and astounding technology will come out of some think tank or scientist's brain, just the way that buying a lottery ticket will solve an individual's financial problems.

In the next 50 years we will have CO_2 concentrations in the atmosphere that have not existed for perhaps a quarter of a billion years. The chances that this will not have an effect on the ecosystem of the Earth, its climate and its future are becoming smaller and smaller with each additional study and research paper. The vast majority of papers and studies seem to tell us it is risky to discount the connection between increasing CO_2 and climate change. The longer we do nothing, ignore the real issues and debate issues that really have little or no effect, the more intractable the problem will become and the more difficult it will be to reverse.

Right now, the levels of CO_2 are the highest in some 650,000 years. In two decades, even if we cut back to 1990 levels, it will be double that. In 50 years it will be so high that some models are saying we could tip over to a runaway greenhouse effect, one that would devastate not only humanity but likely spell the end of 95 percent of species on Earth.

This is not hyperbole. This is a real threat. Even if the chances are one in a hundred that it could occur, I think most people would agree we should plan for ways to make sure it does not happen.

It's Not Going to be Cheap ... The Real Costs

Reducing everything to dollars and cents seems to be a popular way of bringing home ideas. People have a natural affinity for monetarizing pretty much everything, from the effects of hurricanes to the cost of the last stock market crash. Somehow assigning a cost to disaster makes it more real.

How much would it cost to lower the Maritimes ecological footprint, to that of the per capita footprint of Africa? That is a factor of 30. If some miraculous event happened that would allow us to cut our emissions of climate change gases to 3 percent of what we have today, then by extrapolating that figure to the rest of the world, we would be able to live within the Earth's environmental constraints without any deleterious effects.

Heating our homes, transportation and globalized business account for 95 percent of our greenhouse gas emissions. If we used only nuclear, wind, tidal, solar and thermal power to generate electricity we would immediately eliminate 25 percent of the 95 percent. If we redesigned our transportation system to make public transit a viable alternative to the automobile in the 20 largest urban centres, roads, gas and diesel costs, congestion and a host of other transportation plagues would be addressed. Driving a car is one of the greatest expenses that we have in our lives. These relatively small steps would cut our emissions in half and only add about 10 percent to our per capita expenses. With government initiatives and support we could effect a further 10 percent reduction.

If we developed innovations and technology that further reduced the emissions, it would create an industry and business model that could be exported worldwide.

What You Can Do

Small things can have big effects and it is surprising what you can do to make a big difference. The idea is to get your individual ecological footprint as small as possible. You've heard the refrain before but it starts with reducing, reusing and recycling. To begin with, we can all reduce our consumption. Think about reducing your speed in your car, reduce the heating and cooling in your home, reduce what you consume and reduce what you throw out. Keep things longer. Buy locally. What is not shipped reduces the CO_2 output.

Examine what you do, ask questions and educate yourself. In any crisis there are snake oil salesmen who will try to convince you that what they have to offer is the panacea.

Insist that whatever media you subscribe to, whether it is print, television, radio or Internet, have competent people, people who understand the science and the issues behind global warming. It's not enough to approach this from a journalist's perspective; you also have to understand the weight of information and that controversy is not necessarily furthering anything other than ratings. It may be a good strategy journalistically to have two sides to each story, but it may be scientifically inaccurate to portray one approach as equal to another just because they are on opposite sides of an issue.

Intelligent Design is a perfect example of how the media have played into the hands of religious extremists. Intelligent Design is just a variation of the biblical creation myth recorded in Genesis, the first book of the Bible, which says that the world and all its creatures were created in seven days by the supreme being. Christian fundamentalists who subscribe to this idea say this is a scientific theory that should be taught in schools and is on a par with Evolution, which was first proffered by Charles Darwin and Alfred Wallace in the mid-1800s.

In the Maritimes and in all of Canada, Intelligent Design is not part of the course curriculum in any of the public schools. In the United States, fundamentalist groups have been successful in getting it into the curriculum of some states. There is, however, in Canada and in the Maritimes, pressure from these groups to force educators to have Intelligent Design included as an alternative theory to Evolution.

Scientifically, Darwin and Wallace's evolutionary theories are now so firmly proven and accepted by all streams of the scientific community that it would have been unthinkable to assume this bedrock theory could be shaken in the public's mind. But a few astute right-wing creationists have been adept at playing a gullible media, hungry for controversy. Insisting that Intelligent Design be taught in schools as a viable alternative to Wallace and Darwin has undermined the scientific education of young people all across North America.

The same holds true for climate change. Most scientists and climatologists agree that human-induced climate change is happening and provable. Yet just recently Channel Four in the UK aired a documentary about how one group of scientists had proof that climate change was a sham. They asserted there was no connection between the increasing levels of CO_2 and human activity, that rising CO_2 levels are part of a natural cycle. This documentary creates doubt and plays with the facts so as to make it appear there is controversy within the scientific community, when, in fact, the consensus is almost unanimous that climate change is being accelerated by human activities.

Education and understanding how to separate truth from hyperbole is the first and the most important step in figuring out what to do. Once that step has been taken, you can evaluate what works and what doesn't, what makes sense and what doesn't.

One of the great advantages of living in a democracy is that everyone has a voice and a voice that can be effective. The people who make the laws of the land, our political representatives – the MPs, MLAs and councillors of our cities – depend on the feedback they receive from their constituents. A few letters and calls can have an enormous influence. Politicians reflect the will of the people in order to stay in power. That is what they were elected to do. If the environment becomes a priority to constituents, then by proxy it becomes a priority for politicians.

Politically there are options. Not all politicians and political parties are created equal. Many have recently jumped on the eco-bandwagon in an effort to attract the support of voters. It doesn't take much to figure out who is serious and who are the Johnny-come-latelies.

Another avenue is to support local environmental groups who lobby government agencies, groups who collect data and groups who enlist volunteers to make a difference in the environment. Virtually everyone is familiar with the larger, international groups such as Greenpeace and the World Wildlife Fund, but there are also a host of others, many of them regional, provincial and local. Each of these groups is worth exploring and looking at. Clean Nova Scotia and the Ecology Action Centre are a couple from

Nova Scotia. In Prince Edward Island we have PEI Eco-Net and the PEI Environmental Coalition, and in New Brunswick there is the Conservation Council of New Brunswick and the Citizens Coalition for Clean Air. A more comprehensive list can be found in Appendix B.

Talking about climate change, exchanging ideas, even investing in companies which are making a difference environmentally within their sphere of influence and sector are also ways that you can support others who have the same environmental ethic. Visibility is often a large part of the battle. By keeping the environment in the spotlight we make sure that needed changes have the greatest chances of happening.

Lobby to make sure our scientists are funded so they can continue their research and to collect the information we need to make informed and accurate models of what is happening to the climate and the weather. Government funding is limited and most often goes to the squeaky wheel.

Education of our young people has to rate as one of the most effective and important ways that we can plan for the future. The weather and climate problems will have to be addressed by our progeny. Most of the severest and dramatic changes will fall during their lifetimes, not ours. They will be the ones who have to solve the problems we have created. By making sure they have all the educational tools at their disposal, we will give them the best possible opportunities of dealing with the changes that will have to be made.

6

The Future Weather and Climate of the Maritimes

One of the best ways to understand what the computer models say the future of the climate and weather for the Maritimes looks like is from a series of milestones: 10, 25, 50, 100, 1,000 and 15,000 years in the future. These milestones are further broken into two scenarios, the first of which I have called the Good. The second scenario is called the Bad and the Ugly, with apologies to Sergio Leon, Clint Eastwood and Eli Wallach.

The Good

The "Good" scenario is if we are able to get control of our CO_2, nitrous oxide, methane and other GHGs and get them down to 1990 levels in the next ten years (2018). We then make further reductions to get to half the 1990 levels in the next 30 years (2048) and again half in the following 20 years (2068). At these rates we will stabilize at about 700 parts per million, fall short of the runaway greenhouse effect and avoid the number of extinctions and climate changes that the Earth experienced during the Great Dying 250 million years ago.

So here is the "Good" scenario, the one where we do something about our emissions now, where we are able to go beyond the Kyoto Accord and make meaningful changes. I have followed the United Nations' IPCC (Intergovernmental Panel on Climate Change) Report for the most part, but since the report was watered down because of pressure by the United States, China, India and Saudi Arabia, there are some significant differences.

Ten Years From Now (2018)

Ocean Levels: Ten years from now the ocean levels will have risen between 12 to 18 centimetres. As a result, erosion of the softer coastal areas will be an issue. Storm surges will be significantly higher and Prince Edward Island, New Brunswick's Gulf of St. Lawrence and the Bay of Fundy region will feel the effects of waves. Cities like Charlottetown, Summerside and Saint John will be especially vulnerable and feel the changes. Insurance companies will increase the costs of their flood insurance or drop it all together. Older cemeteries too close to the shoreline will have to be relocated. Storm surge breakwalls will have to be increased and in some cases relocated too. Wells along the coasts will become contaminated by salt water. Bridges and other coastal structures will have to be re-engineered to make sure their footings are still able to support the loads as waters rise. Some coastal farms will experience salt water intrusions contaminating the soil.

Greenhouse Gas Levels: Greenhouse gas levels will continue to rise. The curve will become steeper and the levels of CO_2 will rise to about 430 parts per million, even though we will have brought down human greenhouse gas emissions. Methane and other GHGs will continue to rise steeply along this curve as well.

Arctic and Antarctic Melting: The Greenland melt and the western Antarctic ice sheets will be the major global concerns. The Greenland glaciers will be of especially great concern because of the Ocean Conveyor (the Gulf Stream) and its effects on northeastern North America and western Europe. The Greenland melt will have accelerated to roughly five times the 2008 level of 239 cubic kilometres per year to more than 1,000 cubic kilometres. By 2018 the western Antarctic ice sheet melt is also increasing and will be on the verge of collapse.

The Gulf Stream (Part of the Ocean Conveyor): The Gulf Stream will show signs of weakening and fluctuating because of the huge Greenland melt. The warm tropical waters of the Gulf Stream are now spending more time being capped by the less dense, fresher water from the Greenland ice cap and are not warming the northern Atlantic air masses to the extent they did in the previous decade. The offshore surface water temperatures are now cooler than normal for much of the year.

Average Temperatures and Precipitation: The average global temperatures will be half a degree Celsius higher. On the northeastern seaboard of the United States, Canada (Atlantic Canada) and northern Europe we will, however, experience the beginning of a cooler, wetter period. The average temperature is expected to be a quarter of a degree Celsius cooler while the rest of the world, including the interior of North America, has a dramatic warming. That means winter will be wet and slightly longer. The summer months will have more showers and thunderstorms and less sunshine. The winter has more snow and, because of the wilder swings in temperature, more storms. The winter precipitation fluctuates widely between rain and snow.

Immigration: In general, by 2018 many countries are being affected by climate change. Ocean island nations are finding that erosion is a concern as their islands become smaller and more subject to ocean storms and salinity issues. Many peoples have to be resettled and the United Nations is urged to create a panel to deal with climate refugees. Canada in general and the Maritimes in particular, considered to be underpopulated, are pressured to increase climate immigration and refugees.

Ocean Conditions: Storm activity has increased in the Pacific as a new generation of tropical supertyphoons is being created because of the much warmer waters and the more frequent El Niños and La Niñas. In the Atlantic, tropical storms have diminished during the El Niño feedback events, but those that do develop are more likely to be intense. La Niñas tend to make the winters colder and more severe in North America. Average ocean temperature has increased by half a degree Celsius.

Ecosystems: At first, as climate change took hold, the Maritimes experienced insect invasions of species commonly found farther south. This has relaxed somewhat as the climate has cooled. In the ocean waters, however, the changes in temperature and salinity have displaced many of the species traditionally found in the Maritimes waters, and in general, because conditions are fluctuating, new species have as yet not moved into the empty niches.

Agriculture: Not much has changed in agriculture. Heavy rainfall and snowfall has offset increased evaporation rates, so a sort of status quo has been maintained.

Forests: Because the weather has become stormier and wetter, with a slight decline in average temperatures, the forests continue to be predominantly conifers. The growth rates remain pretty much the same as they have been in previous decades. Invasive pests, though, have taken their toll and established themselves due to climate change. Because of the dry tinder created by the insect pests and the increased frequency of summer thunder and lightning storms, forest fires are more frequent and fiercer.

Winter and Summer: Winter has become longer again, though it is wetter and with more snowfall. The average temperature is back to 1990 levels, after a shorter period of increase. There are also more storms because the rest of the world continues to heat up. While the North Atlantic is cooler, the fact that melt continues in Greenland makes the temperatures between the summer and winter seasons in the Maritimes greater. Storms in general last longer and are more severe.

Summer is shorter, wetter and cooler. There are more storms as the hot humid air from the south collides with the cold air of the North Atlantic. Cold fronts produce more violent lightning and thunderstorms, more often.

Storms and Hurricanes: In general, the Maritimes are embarking on a stormier regime of weather. Though there has been a damping of the hurricane season because of the protracted warming in the Pacific and the increased El Niño frequency, the tropical storms that form are stronger and larger. Those hurricanes that find their way into Maritime waters get an additional energy boost from frontal disturbances, making them faster, larger and stronger.

Twenty-Five Years From Now (2033)

Globally: Twenty-five years from now all governments, businesses and individuals are aware the climate has changed. Satellite and computer technology have irrefutably proven that climate change has been enhanced to a significant degree by human activity. We have been able to turn back from the brink of global climate disaster, though the war is not yet won. There are still many hurdles, but we have had some very significant successes. This is the state of affairs in 2033.

CO_2 and other greenhouse gas emissions have been reduced to half the 1990 levels. Carbon sequestering, a reality for more than a decade, has enabled China, the United States and India to utilize their huge coal reserves without adding significantly to CO_2 and other GHGs. The GHGs increase continues, but the hockey stick-shaped curve, the exponential increase that Al Gore showed in his documentary, *An Inconvenient Truth*, has levelled off.

Nuclear power has now been brought on line with smaller fourth-generation reactors. New technologies have made the reactors the most reliable technology on the planet. The reactors are smaller, enabling individual cities and communities to construct them and generate as much as 50 percent of the energy needed. The radiation issue has been pretty much solved. New technology has allowed for the drilling of ultra deep holes into the Earth's crust. A combination of a deep subterranean nuclear blast and the almost simultaneous pouring of 20 million tonnes of molten iron into the fissure has allowed the nuclear waste to be buried into the magma of the Earth's mantle. The mantle is already radioactive and what is buried there will never come to the surface. In addition, new geothermal power sources have been unleashed as a byproduct of the technology. Nuclear power helps augment the nascent hydrogen economy, splitting water into hydrogen and oxygen to provide a portable energy source to power a much cleaner transportation infrastructure.

Human population has also levelled off and is now at nine billion. China, India and the United States are the world's most populous countries with a combined population of four billion people.

The equatorial region has continued to warm and the climate models show that even as the human CO_2 level input has levelled off, the effects of the GH gases will continue for another thousand years.

The Greenland ice cap has continued to melt and only 75 percent of the 2008 ice cap is left. What used to be one of the harshest climates in the world is now warmer and habitable along the coastal areas. Vast parts of the island are now becoming exposed as torrents of fresh water pour off the huge glaciers.

Ocean Levels: Twenty-five years from now the ocean levels around the world will have risen between 30 and 60 centimetres. All regions of the world are now plagued with eroding shorelines and floods in places where floods didn't previously happen.

In the Maritimes, the time for drastic action and planning has come. Berms and dikes hold off the rising waters in some places. But the softer, sandier, low-sloping shores are a problem. Here flood plains extend kilometres and surround huge once livable areas with water. Beaches are shifting as storms and higher water levels change the coastline. The coastal cities of Charlottetown, Summerside, Saint John, Moncton, Halifax, Sydney, Yarmouth, Truro and others all feel the impact. Charlottetown and other cities with softer, low-incline shores, have now introduced a policy of resettlement. The accelerating rise of the waters and storms have convinced local, regional and central officials that moving is the best option.

Greenhouse Gas Levels: Greenhouse gas levels continue to rise, but the steep rise has now turned shallower. The total amount of GHGs going into the atmosphere is still too high, but almost under control. GHGs have not been this high since the Mesozoic era when CO_2 levels created a world with no permanent ice caps and dinosaurs dominated the world.

At this rate, the global concentration will level off below the critical runaway point of 900 parts per million. Climate change is still underway, but the very worst scenarios are now falling away. The current amount of CO_2 in the atmosphere is just under 750 parts per million, roughly twice the 2008 levels.

Arctic and Antarctic Melting: Much of Greenland's coastline has now been exposed by the retreating glaciers. Almost 500 cubic kilometres of water are pouring annually into the North

Atlantic. Plants, especially trees, are beginning to make a toehold in the southern regions for the first time in 120,000 years. The western Antarctic ice sheet continues to hold up, though major portions now appear to be threatened. The eastern Antarctic sheet is remaining stable.

The Gulf Stream (Part of the Ocean Conveyor): The fresh water from Greenland is the major concern for countries bounding the North Atlantic. The cold fresh water continues to cap the warm, saline flows from the south, keeping the transfer of heat from taking place. As a result, in the UK the Thames has frozen over for the first time in 200 years, there is skating on the canals in the Netherlands and in the Maritimes of Canada the winter is longer and colder than it has been for a generation.

Researchers are now quite concerned that the fresh water influx will mean the Gulf Stream will shut down. The amount of heat energy transferred through the Gulf Stream is enormous and has kept the North Atlantic warm for millennia.

The Gulf Stream fresh water capping has also meant a transition in the species that have traditionally been found off the Maritimes.

Average Temperatures and Precipitation: The average global temperature is now 30 degrees warmer, though the North Atlantic, Gulf Stream-influenced regions continue to be cooler. The Arctic and Antarctic regions continue to warm the most quickly.

Immigration: Climate immigration is now recognized as a worldwide phenomenon. The United Nations has instituted a complex plan for member nations to deal with the issue. Refugees whose homes have been flooded by rising waters or dessicated by desertification are being resettled in places where the warming has created new areas to settle. Among the sought-after areas of the world for new settlers are Siberia, northern Canada, Greenland and, most surprisingly, the western Antarctic. All these areas have benefitted from retreating ice, new unsettled exposed land and more benign weather. This may be the last great migration of humanity, as people flee the rapid climate changes.

Ocean Conditions: Storms continue to wreak havoc. Tropical storms in all oceans are bigger and more severe. A new change in the ocean is its vertical temperature profile and its attendant effects. For much of the past ten million years the abyssal deep waters have been cold, near $0°C$. As the atmosphere warms it has also warmed the ocean waters to a greater depth. In some coastal areas, this warming has extended to the ocean bottom and modified the great ocean currents that circle the world.

Methane hydrate at the bottom of the oceans is now being released in small quantities, bubbling up to the surface. While much of the emphasis has been focused on the impact of carbon dioxide, methane is a very important greenhouse gas. Methane release from the ocean bottom is now becoming a climate change issue.

In addition to methane, studies are also showing that the average global ocean temperatures mean the waters are unable to absorb as much carbon dioxide and, in fact, are releasing CO_2 into the atmosphere, offsetting the reductions that have been made to human CO_2 emissions.

Ecosystems: Life is changing in the oceans. In addition to some negative impacts, such as the disappearance and migration of traditional species, there are also some positive changes. As the waters in the southern Maritimes warm, oceanographers are detecting new reef growth. This reef growth is able to absorb atmospheric CO_2 and in part offsets the ocean's diminished ability to absorb CO_2.

Winter and Summer: The seasons have continued their cooling in the Maritimes. The summer remains stormier, with less sunshine and more frequent unsettled weather. The winter remains variable and cool. The total amount of snowfall has increased, though much of the snow that falls soon melts and does not accumulate. The onset of spring is now pushed back two weeks and the gains made during the first decade of 2000 have now been erased.

Storms and Hurricanes: Storms and hurricanes remain a significant issue and plague the east coast. Hurricanes routinely make their way into northern waters and regions in spite of the fact that the climate in the northeast is cooler than it used to be. The extratropical transition effect is pronounced and gives hurricanes a significant boost when they head north.

Winter storms over the North Atlantic continue to be long-lasting and severe. The North Atlantic waters are among the stormiest in the world and a significant threat to industry and shipping. When the winter storms edge close to the coast, their strong central low pressure brings in extremely cold arctic air, held in place by strong continental ridges of high pressure.

In addition to larger cyclonic winter and summer storm systems, frontal supercells generated by the leading edges of cold fronts during the summer months continue to provide thunder and lightning storms. Wind, hail, lightning and heavy torrential rains have become a fact of life and low-lying inland areas experience their harmful effects.

Fifty Years From Now (2058)

The world is a dramatically different place. The effects of the past two centuries of population growth and environment degradation have taken their toll. The world population has levelled off at eleven billion and many regions of the globe are covered by supercities merging into one another. The entire eastern coast of the United States and southern Ontario is one vast city running from Atlanta to Boston and inland through the Great Lakes region from Montreal to Toronto to Chicago.

The climate of southern and central North America has changed dramatically and become hotter. On average the climate is warmer by six degrees Celsius than during 2008. Heat waves and droughts remain a major concern and each summer thousands suffer from a variety of heat-induced ailments. Death tolls are highest among the infirm and the elderly. Winter has retreated and is a full month shorter than it was in 2008.

Human-induced GHG emissions are now under control and increases are mainly due to natural processes. The main additions of GHGs come from the oceans which, due to their warmer conditions, cannot hold as much dissolved CO_2 as they could in 2008. Methane outbursts from methane hydrate, while not common, have occurred and continue to be a threat as the temperature profile of the oceans changes and warms.

The Greenland ice cap is now half of what it was in 2008. The melt has peaked and has begun to diminish. Much of the continued melt is now absorbed into new lakes that are forming inland, and only about half the amount of fresh water is flowing into the North Atlantic as in 2033. As a result, the Gulf Stream has begun to resurge and warm northern Europe and eastern North America. The slowing and occasional stopping of the Gulf Stream has decreased in frequency. Global warming has increased around the rest of the world and has now begun in the Maritimes. It is going catch up quickly.

In the Antarctic, the western ice sheet has fractured and broken off in many places, though the bulk of the sheet still remains. Consequently, ocean water levels are a full metre higher than in 2008, though if the western sheet breaks off that will change dramatically. The eastern ice sheet in the Antarctic has held and in the past two decades has neither diminished nor increased. The cold melt from the western sheet has actually increased the snowfall over the continent, keeping the ocean levels from rising catastrophically.

In the Maritimes, flooding, rising ocean levels and turbulent weather have taken their toll. Prince Edward Island and the Bay of Fundy have seen their coastlines altered and the major shore cities relocated to less vulnerable, higher ground.

Agriculture has resurged because of the warming, though the Maritimes are still not self-sufficient in food supply. But the Maritimes are able to export water, wind and tidal energy and hydrogen to the vast North American market. In spite of cooler weather and increased storm activity, the Maritimes have had a fast increase in population as the interior of North America has warmed. Places like southern Arizona are experiencing a drought not seen in thousands of years. Much of the US heartland agri- culture has shifted northwards into Canada. But water remains an issue. Because of water concerns in most of central North America, the population is now moving to regions where water is more plentiful.

The Maritimes are a haven for eco-refugees, in spite of the fact the weather has become more turbulent. Though the weather on the whole has been cooler and wetter, it has also brought abundant fresh water. Water is the new oil and as a net exporter, the Maritimes have tapped into a new economy.

One Hundred Years From Now (2108)

The world has learned a great deal from the climate change crisis and has weathered the storm, though millions upon mil- lions of people have been displaced and even died because of the rapid changes to lifestyle and habitat. The oceans are now three metres higher and a map of the world shows that many of the places that were above sea level are now eroded and gone. The eastern seaboard of the United States and Canada has changed because of higher sea levels. The shallow, sandy coastlines of Florida, Louisiana and Prince Edward Island are especially vul- nerable to erosion and will experience even greater changes in the coming decades.

One-quarter of the species of the Earth that were alive in 2008 are now extinct. Forests have changed in content and extent. Deciduous trees dominate the Maritimes and conifers have died out. The Ocean Conveyor is now back to transporting warm saline water and its energy to the North Atlantic. The population of the Earth has now begun to decline, and is now at eight billion.

The Maritimes are a dynamic hub and contribute to the have-nots of the world, including the once rich provinces of Canada, such as Ontario. Ontario has suffered greatly because of climate change. The Great Lakes have declined to less than half their extent as a combination of evaporation, reduced precipitation and water usage has depleted them. Water, once considered to be so abundant in the Great Lakes, has become a valued and precious commodity. Glacial water, left over from the last glacial advances, is now all gone. The Ogallala Aquifer is now dry, the mighty Colorado River a trickle and the millions of lakes through the Canadian Shield have dried up.

CO_2 has been stabilized at 800 parts per million and will remain there for another few hundred years before the natural processes begin to wind back the concentrations.

This is the peak of the interglacial. Though the changes are not ending, the worst of the crisis has been dealt with successfully.

One Thousand Years From Now (3008)

The CO_2 levels are now back to 350 parts per million, where they were in the 1990s. Greenland has been free of ice for 500 years. In Antarctica, the western ice sheet collapsed, though the eastern ice sheet remained intact. As a result, ocean levels have risen fifteen metres with predictable results.

The runaway greenhouse effect never did happen and the Earth, while it did have greenhouse gas levels not seen for millions of years, could have been worse off. The CO_2 crisis has delayed the onset of the normal cycle of ice ages by almost 700 years. The cycle is now back on track.

The Earth's population has declined to a stable and sustainable 250 million individuals, living in a diminished though still vibrant ecosystem. It is a vast utopia, where conflict and obfuscation have given way to fact and a virtually ideal world.

Humanity, however, will have another problem to deal with as a new ice advance takes hold.

Fifteen Thousand Years From Now (17008)

From space the Earth is brilliant. The white ice sheets of the north cover much of North America, Europe and Asia. Antarctica has reassumed its crystalline mantle. The ice has come back, the oceans declined and the continental shelves have grown again. At night the twinkle of cities can still be seen from space. Humanity has survived and weathered both global warming and cooling, and the ecosystems have begun their slow recovery and evolution into the future.

The Bad and The Ugly

This is a scenario that I hope we can avoid. It is a story of failure and of disaster, of suffering on a scale never before experienced. It is also a story of greed and sadness.

"The Bad and The Ugly" scenario, at first, does not seem so different from the "Good" scenario. But as the years pass, it quickly becomes apparent that a threshold, a tipping point, has been passed and the changes are like a runaway train. Once this happens, the process cannot be halted or even slowed. No amount of effort or investment can pull us back. The scenario is now unstoppable and has a life of its own until it is played out.

It, of course, begins with the continuation of the process that we deal with on a daily basis, the triangle of personal, governmental and business interests. The debate has shifted from denying that the climate is changing. Evidence that the climate is changing is everywhere and obvious. The newer argument against action and cutbacks in greenhouse gases is that this is all a natural process of the environment and human actions play no role.

The conjecture that follows is the result of delaying our actions in reducing human greenhouse gas emissions.

Ten Years From Now (2018)

The world has not been able to agree on what to do about the emissions of greenhouse gases. Coal, oil and other fossil fuels still dominate the energy spectrum. Though some countries have been successful in implementing clean technologies, population controls and cutbacks in carbon emissions, by and large, it is business as usual. The levels, globally, of CO_2 are at a level of 450 parts per million. CO_2 is increasing by more than 50 parts per million per decade and is rising.

The Greenland melt is putting over 1,000 cubic kilometres of fresh water per year into the North Atlantic. This has had a major effect on the Gulf Stream, which has slowed down and stopped for days at a time, causing great concern. The climate in the Maritimes, northeastern United States and northwestern Europe has become colder, with increased snowfalls and precipitation and stormier weather, despite the fact that the rest of the world is experiencing a generally hotter climate.

The western Antarctic ice sheet has calved some enormous ice flows into the ocean waters around Antarctica. The western half of the continent is experiencing heavier snowfalls and its ice sheet is actually growing, while the eastern ice sheet melt has begun to flow faster into the ocean, balancing the increased snowfall. A few of the icebergs are as large as small countries and have made the southern ocean waters around Antarctica a minefield of ice.

The ocean levels are now 30 centimetres higher than they were in 2008. Flooding in many of the small, low-lying islands around the world is now a reality. Storm surges have flooded the Truro, PEI and Bay of Fundy areas and the various levels of government have now begun to look at subsidies and solutions to the rising waters.

While the east looks at a resurgence of colder, wetter weather, the interior of North America bakes and becomes drier. The Great Lakes are at their lowest levels ever because of increased evaporation and reduced winter seasons and ice cover. Most of the myriad of small lakes in the Canadian Shield are also facing lower levels from a longer warm season, which increases evaporation. Once gone, the water in these lakes can take as long as 300 years to replace. We must consider our water to be non-renewable, just as finite as our fish and other natural resources.

The massive mountain glaciers of the Rockies are now pretty much gone. Their melt has increased exponentially, accelerating to the point where the last of the ice sheets that provided water to communities and nature for hundreds of years have almost disappeared.

The reserves of glacial water in the aquifers, lakes, streams and mountains are now used solely for human consumption, with the predictable effects on the ecosystems. The midwest is drying at a phenomenal rate and climatologists are predicting a massive central North American drought that could last decades, if not longer.

In the winter, in Atlantic Canada, snowfalls are more fre-quent and heavier. Snowfalls of more than 50 centimetres occur often. The winter is longer and though there are melts during the winter, the snow is sticking around longer. Travel is more difficult. Municipalities are spending much more on keeping the roads clear. The wear and tear on the roads and bridges is higher so maintenance is needed more frequently. Costs of food, goods and business have increased because of the weather. The upside is that while much of North America has to deal with drier con-ditions, the Maritimes has no shortage of water.

Farms have had to change to more durable crops and live-stock as the weather has become harsher.

Twenty-Five Years From Now (2033)

The world has recognized there is indeed a change happening and that the scientists were right in the first place. Massive efforts to undo the changes that have transpired since 1990 are underway. But there is a cruel reality playing out. Here are the facts.

The global population is ten billion. The battle for water, land and air has begun in earnest. Canada, in signing the North America Free Trade Agreement (NAFTA) with the United States, is locked into massive diversion projects to supply water to a desperate Southwest.

Russia has starved Europe for food, resources and power and its almost one billion people are watching their standard of living plummet. Once the envy of the world, countries like Germany and France contend with summer heat and drought and watch slums grow in all their major cities.

Hundreds of thousands now die each summer in the incredible heat waves that strike central Europe, while the northwest contends with the onslaught of increased winter storms and heavier snowfalls as the Gulf Stream shuts down. The Gulf Stream has reduced the amount of heat it transfers to the north by almost 40 percent, because of fresh water from the Greenland ice cap. It has modified climate in all countries bounding the North Atlantic.

The biggest news is the eastern ice sheet has begun to collapse in the Antarctic. It is expected that in ten years water levels around the world will rise five metres because of the Greenland and Antarctic ice melt. Unless there is a technological miracle that can be applied, the ice will collapse and melt with catastrophic repercussions. The coastlines will alter as never before and tens, if not hundreds, of millions of people will be affected.

On the east coast of North America, much of Prince Edward Island will disappear, along with drastic changes to Halifax, Moncton, Saint John, Truro, the Annapolis Valley, the Saint John River Valley and coastline along the Gulf of St Lawrence. But this is a drop in the proverbial bucket when compared to what will happen to the coast of the United States.

Governments, instead of reducing CO_2 and other greenhouse gas emissions, are proposing that solar blockages, ocean seeding and other bizarre technological solutions be implemented. The inaction for the past 25 years has pushed CO_2 levels to almost 700 parts per million. Scientists expect the tipping point of 900 parts per million will be reached by 2058. Modelling and studies indicate that this is the level of no return. Governments decide to pursue these limited and unlikely options because even if emissions were reduced to zero immediately, natural processes, methane hydrate evaporation, cloud cover, changes in Arctic and Antarctic albedo and agricultural gas additions will push us over the limit of 900 parts per million.

Flooding and storms are more frequent and violent all around the world. The major deserts of Africa, North America, Asia and Australia are drier and hotter. Temperatures have now climbed by five degrees Celsius around the world and by seven degrees in the Arctic and Antarctic.

As the north polar regions are ice-free during the summer months, political and military jockeying takes place among the circumpolar nations. Canada becomes a proxy for the US in its dispute with Russia and even China, which has desperate water shortages.

Even though the Arctic of Canada is warming, the agriculture that has been lost in the southern prairies, Ontario and Quebec due to water concerns does not migrate to the north because the glaciation of the past three million years stripped all the soil from the Canadian Shield. The heat and dryness has exacerbated soil erosion and millions of hectares of valuable topsoil is lost.

Fifty Years From Now (2058)

The short, cold respite generated by the shutdown of the Gulf Stream portion of the Ocean Conveyor has peaked and now is declining. The Maritimes are warming. The ocean levels have risen ten metres as the Antarctic ice collapse is making a huge contribution to water levels. Greenland is now virtually free of permanent ice.

The island archipelago in the north is free of summer ice. Trees are beginning to grow, and other plants and animals are beginning to occupy the vacated niches left by the massive extinctions of most of the Arctic flora and fauna.

Extinctions have become a fact of life all around the world. In the Maritimes the resurgence of the Gulf Stream has pushed the remaining indigenous species into the far north. The ocean is now home to starfish, bivalves, sea cucumbers and algae as fish and mammals that were once almost without number disappear. Forests are experiencing a massive die off. Conifers are being replaced by broad-leafed plants. Insects are also invading, adding to the changes in the ecosystems.

Storms begin in earnest. The changes of season bring no respite to the almost non-stop storm activity. Flooding, surges and storms with torrential downpours are now taxing every government. Large migrations are taking place all over the globe and power struggles have become innumerable with the attendant loss of life, as refugees drain our technological resources.

One Hundred Years From Now (2108)

The world is politically and economically on the verge of collapse. The tipping point has been passed. A runaway greenhouse effect is rapidly overtaking the Earth.

CO_2 is at 1,000 parts per million, the global temperature is warmer by fifteen degrees Celsius, the ice caps in the north have melted, the eastern sheet in the Antarctic has collapsed, the western sheet is now melting, the Ocean Conveyor is regenerating in the North Atlantic and global warming is catching up with the Maritimes.

The ocean levels are 20 metres higher and rising quickly. The death tolls defy number. Extinctions of animals and plants are widespread. Agriculture is unable to keep pace with the changes. Civilization is now shrinking, and the strong are hoarding and circling the wagons. War over resources increases the death toll.

One Thousand Years From Now (3008)

The ecosystem has collapsed. People are extinct along with their much vaunted civilization and 95 percent of all species have died out. The average global temperature is an unbelievable 40°C. The oceans are effervescing CO_2, methane and hydrogen sulfide. No ice is to be found anywhere on the Earth, other than on the peaks of a few very high mountains.

The CO_2 levels are at 5,000 parts per million.

The ocean levels are 120 metres higher than they are today.

The Earth's hyperwarmth will last for an estimated one million years, before the global cycles of ice ages return. This time the Earth will be a lesser place. It will take three to five million years for the niches to begin to be occupied again and new species to populate the land, air and sea.

The Uncertainties

Of course the future is not certain. What I have outlined in this chapter is an educated guess as to what might happen to us and the world we live in. It may well be there are more than the two possibilities I have delineated and that the reality is different from either. But as far as I can see, either we will solve this crisis or we will not, and we have at best another decade of inaction before the decision is taken from us and what we have set in motion becomes an uncontrollable juggernaut.

The questions, the uncertainties, are more to do with us as individuals. Can we muster the will to do something and make the climate change issue the paramount issue of our times, putting into place meaningful actions that will solve the crisis?

Another uncertainty is the placement of the tipping point. At what level of CO_2 and other climate change gases will the process become runaway – that is, become so large that we are unable to stop the warming? When will the decision to do something and our ability to stop climate change be taken away from us?

Models are models and only as good as the information and the amount of investment that we make in trying to get the information. If we stop our research or the collection of the raw data or put our research resources elsewhere, then we limit our ability to understand and know what will happen.

What is also uncertain is the response that climate change will trigger. Wars have been fought over countless things. To suppose that we will be any different in the future as the environment begins to degrade substantially and water, air, land and the ecosystem become valuable and sought-after commodities is open to question. Without planning and organizations to help with the rapid changes that are expected to happen, we will be at risk of losing much that we have built up over the past few centuries.

Addressing the Naysayers

This is the first thing that must be done. Our crisis is too dire to be left to the news services or the need for entertainment or conjecture. We must bring personal, political and business will in line and begin to tackle the problem on all levels. The scientific consensus is there and it's unequivocal.

Science has in recent years become a bit of a pariah. Even though medicine, agriculture, our industries and standard of living are all based on the incredible method of science, articulate and intelligent people with other agendas have been able to resurrect superstition, fables and myth, bringing them back into the mainstream of culture and thought.

Countering mystification and misinformation about climate change will require an effort from not only business and governments, but from the individual as well. Education and a grounding in the basics of science are absolutely necessary in order for the coming changes to be understood. If we act without understanding, the precious resources that are so limited will be wasted. All the significant advances that we have made as a culture and people have been made through the power of science.

Once information has been collected and peer-reviewed, it is suitable to use as public information and becomes part of our platform of understanding. As we as individuals begin to understand the circumstances of global warming we can then expect others to do the same. We can hold the media to a higher level of understanding and demand that they not react and publicize something that is wrong or incorrect, without first investigating and understanding.

A counterpoint is only valid in a peer review. People who do not have the information basics are rarely able to make any meaningful contribution in science. All the debate in the world by journalists has never advanced science. Climate science is no different than nuclear science.

For example, the media cannot determine whether quantum mechanics is a valid theory. Nor can they make any contribution to whether it in fact describes the universe correctly. Their articles about quantum mechanics can, only in the most basic terms, describe the overview of the theory. It is only the scientists who, when they publish their papers for other scientists to review, can make any serious changes and modifications to the theory.

This is not elitist. This is true and has been true for 500 years. We are in the same position that Copernicus, Galileo, Bruno and a host of other scientists were during the Renaissance against the juggernaut of the Catholic Church. They were advancing ideas that were based in observation and testing through peer-reviewed publication. They were up against a powerful and often dangerous body of rhetoric that had its basis outside observation, one that used revelation as its platform. No amount of wishing, hoping and believing could change the observations, recording of facts and peer review. No amount of trying to reconcile the two methods has ever been able to undo the method of science. Science and scientific method are, in all the years that humanity has existed, the only body that has lifted the veil of superstition and ignorance from our eyes. It is a method that has given us our technology and our civilization. Now we have to rely on it to save our civilization.

Through education and a basic grounding in science, we can very quickly stop the misinformation and rhetoric designed to advance a particular bias. By expecting those who give us information, and publicize and disseminate stories about science, to be equally grounded we can halt almost all the deliberate confusion.

Thinking Versus Believing

This is a crucial point. Science is not a matter of belief. The scientific investigation of the global warming crisis is all about science: the collection, interpretation and review of the information and then designing the theories that best explain all the information collected. Belief will not make one iota of difference in whether there is or is not a global warming issue, any more than believing that the positions of the stars will influence the outcome of people's lives. Debate, solutions, conjecture all have to take place from within the confines of science and scientific method. Anything else will doom us.

To say that I believe global warming will be accelerated because of human activities is a misstatement. After looking at all the studies, the reviews between scientists, using my understanding of science and scientific method, it is my thinking that leads to my opinion that climate change, global warming created by human activities, is a fact, a reality. So belief has nothing to do with it. I do not believe in climate change at all. I think that climate change is upon us because of our activities.

Not Being Overwhelmed

It is still not too late. We can make meaningful changes as long as we do not procrastinate. We still have a little time.

The major issues are fossil fuels, consumption and our population. We burn too much fossil fuel – coal, oil and natural gas. We consume too many resources, and there are too many of us on the planet. These are substantial problems, massive and daunting. But, and this is a big but, we can effect changes, if we want to. The problem is no different than the one we faced during the Renaissance. The changes in thinking and understanding led to our civilization and prosperity. It was a monumental shift that allowed Newton, Einstein, Faraday, Bohr and a host of scientists who changed the world to add to the vast amount of understanding we have today. The first scientists were up against a powerful body. But they were not overwhelmed. They were in search of the truth and it was their guide.

Many people I have spoken to are of the opinion that their actions do not matter. Quite to the contrary, the actions of the individual are paramount. For example, if for two generations, we all decided that the population of humans was too great and we had only one child per couple, our population would in short order decline precipitously. Taking into account the first and second generations would still be alive while the third was being born, there would be an increase in population for a couple of decades, but after the initial increase it would rapidly fall to a fraction of what it is today. In 100 years we could cut our population to a quarter of what it is now. And even if we made no other changes to our lifestyles as far as consumption and energy usage was concerned, our global emissions would drop 75 percent from 2008 levels! In 100 years our population would be where it was at the beginning of the First World War and the potential for a much better environment and lifestyle would be accessible to everyone on Earth. It would be a place where everyone could have pretty much anything they wanted. Poverty, extinction, wars, space, water problems, air pollution would all cease to be an issue. Sounds like utopia and a pipe dream, but it is accessible.

This is an example of what individuals can do and how they do not need governments, businesses or any other organizations to come up with drastic solutions, laws and restrictions to make a difference to global warming. A simple solution is at hand. It's just whether we want, as individuals, to implement the solution for a much better world tomorrow. And this is just one example, one small solution where the individual can make a resounding and spectacular difference.

There are other solutions as well. But we each have to make them. We cannot rely on waiting for others to comply before we decide to make the changes. It starts in Charlottetown and Halifax and Charlo, with individuals. If that can be effected, then we have a chance at averting the worst.

Appendix A

Some of the Milestones
that Mark the Life History of Earth

(Ma = Millions of years ago)

4,000 Ma earliest biogenic carbon

3,800 Ma banded iron formations (with reduced iron)

3,700 Ma oldest rocks

3,500 Ma oldest stromatolites (a symbiotic culture of cyanbacteria and blue-green algae that is the signature fossil of the Precambrian)

3,500 Ma first evidence of sex

3,450 Ma earliest bacteria

3,000 Ma earliest Precambrian ice ages

[?] Chuos Tillites of southwest Africa (Tillites are sedimentary deposits that are evidence of massive glaciation during a time when Earth was covered in ice, a time now called Snowball Earth.)

[?] Sturtian Tillites of the Finders Range, south-central Australia

3,000 Ma earliest photosynthetic bacteria

2,700 Ma oldest chemical evidence of complex cells

2,300 Ma first green algae (eukaryotes)

2,000 Ma free oxygen in the atmosphere

2,000 Ma to 1600 Ma Gowganda tillites in the Canadian shield

1,700 Ma end of the banded iron formations and red beds
become abundant (non-reducing atmosphere)

700 Ma first metazoans late Proterozoic (Ediacaran Epoch) –
first skeletons

570 Ma to present Phanerozoic Eon

100 Ma development of the angiosperms (flowering plants)

2 Ma to present modern world and humans' appearance on earth

0.01 Ma end of the last ice age

0.001 Ma warming trend of the middle ages

0.0001 Ma end of the mini ice age

Appendix B

A Short List of Environmental Groups in the Maritime Provinces

Nova Scotia

Atlantic First Nations Environmental Network – www.afnen.ca

Atlantic Society of Fish and Wildlife Biologists – www.chebucto.ns.ca/environment/asfwb

Bay of Fundy Ecosystem Partnership – www.bofep.org

Blomidon Naturalist's Society – www.blomindonnaturalists.ca

Canadian Parks and Wilderness Society – www.cpaws.org

Clean Nova Scotia Foundation – www.clean.ns.ca

Coastal Coalition Nova Scotia – www.ccns.chebucto.org

Coastal Communities Network of Nova Scotia – www.coastalcommunities.ns.ca

Discovery Centre – www.discoverycentre.ns.ca

Ecology Action Centre – www.ecologyaction.ca

Environment Guidelines –
    www.cnsopb.ns.ca/environment/guidelines.html

Federation of Nova Scotia Naturalists –
    www.chebucto.ns.ca/environment/fnsn

Friends of Hemlock Ravine –
    www.chebucto.ns.ca/environment/cpaws/fhr/

Friends of McNab's Island Society – www.mcnabsisland.ca

Friends of Point Pleasant Park –
    www.chebucto.ns.ca/Environment/FPPP/

Halifax Field Naturalists – www.hfn.chebucto.org

Natural History Resources –
    www.chebucto.ns.ca/environment/nhr/index.html

Nova Scotia Bird Society – www.nsbs.chebucto.org

Nova Scotia Environment and Development Coalition –
    www.chebucto.ns.ca/environment/nsedc/

Nova Scotia Herpetofaunal Atlas Project –
    www.landscape.acadiau.ca/herpatlas

Nova Scotia Museum of Natural History –
    www.museum.gov.ns.ca/mnh/

Nova Scotia Nature Trust – www.nsnt.ca

Nova Scotia Plant Savers – www.avalongardens.ca/nsps

Nova Scotia Public Interest Research Group – www.nspirg.org

Solar Nova Scotia – www.solarns.ca

St. Georges Bay Ecosystem Project –
    www.stfx.ca/research/gbayesp/

Tobeatic Wilderness Committee – www.tobeaticwilderness.ca

New Brunswick

Association de la protection du bassin versant de la Bouctouche
www.nben.ca/egroups/findgroups/indexframe_findgroups.htm

Atlantic Salmon Federation – www.asf.ca

Atlantic Wildlife Institute – www.atlanticwildlife.ca

Bathurst Sustainable Development –
www.bathurstsustainabledevelopment.com

Canadian Organic Growers, NB Chapter –
www.cog.ca/nb/index/htm

Canadian Parks and Wilderness Society, NB Chapter –
www.cpawsnb/org

Cape Jourimain Nature Centre – www.capejourimain.ca/

Citizen's Coalition for Clean Air –
www.sjfn.nb.ca/community_hall/c/citixxxx.html

Conservation Council of New Brunswick –
www.conservationcouncil.ca

EOS Eco-Energy – www.eos-eco.net

Falls Brook Centre – www.fallsbrookcentre.ca

Meduxnekeag River Association –
www.web.net/~meduxnekeag/index.htm

Nature Conservancy of Canada – www.natureconservancy.ca

New Brunswick Federation of Naturalists – www.naturenb.ca

People Against Nuclear Energy – www.citizen.org/cmep/energy_
enviro_nuclear/nuclear_power_plants/

Sentinelles Petitcodiac Riverkeeper – www.petitcodiac.org

Sierra Club of Canada, Atlantic Canada Chapter –
www.sierraclub.ca/atlantic

SOS Eau Water Sankwan – www.sosews.ca

Tantramar Watershed Committee – www.tantramarwatershed.org

UNB Environmental Society – www.unbf.ca/clubs/ENVS

Prince Edward Island

Canadian Environmental Network – www.cen-rce.org

Directory of PEI Environmental Groups –
www.earthdirectory.net/canada

MacPhail Woods Ecological Forestry Project –
www.macphailwoods.org

Organic PEI – www.organicpei.com

PEI Eco-Net – www.isn.net/~network

PEI Environmental Coalition – www.ecopei.ca

Southeast Environmental Association – www.seapei.ca

UPEI Energy Awareness Program –
www.upei.ca/energyawareness

Appendix C

Bibliography

Alley, Richard B. *The Two-Mile Time Machine: Ice Cores, Abrupt Climate Change, and Our Future*. Princeton, New Jersey: Princeton University Press, 2000.

Bell, Art and Whitley Strieber. *The Coming Global Superstorm*. New York: Pocket Books, Simon and Shuster, 2000.

Davis, Devra. *When Smoke Ran Like Water: Tales of Environmental Deception and the Battle Against Pollution*. New York: Basic Books, 2002.

Davis, Mike. *Planet of Slums*. London: Verso, 2006.

DeVilliers, Marq. *Windswept: The Story of Wind and Weather.* Toronto: McClelland and Stewart, 2006.

Dewdney, A.K. *Beyond Reason: 8 Great Problems that Reveal the Limits of Science*. Hoboken, New Jersey: John Wiley and Sons Inc., 2004.

Diamond, Jared. *Collapse: How Societies Choose to Fail or Survive*. London: Penguin Group, 2005.

Diamond, Jared. *Guns, Germs and Steel: The Fates of Human Societies.* New York: WW Norton and Company, 1997.

Eldredge, Niles. *The Miner's Canary: Unravelling the Mysteries of Extinction.* UK: Virgin Books, 1991.

Fagan, Brian. *The Little Ice Age: How Climate Made History 1300-1850.* New York: Basic Books, 2000.

Flannery, Tim. *The Weather Makers: The History and Future Impact of Climate Change.* Melbourne, Australia: Text Publishing, 2005.

Glen, William. *Mass Extinction Debates: How Science Works in a Crisis.* Stanford, California: Stanford University Press, 1994.

Gribbon, John. *Hothouse Earth: The Greenhouse Effect and Gaia.* New York: Grove Weidenfeld, 1990.

Hallam, A. and P.B. Wignall. *Mass Extinctions and Their Aftermath.* Oxford: Oxford University Press, 1997.

Hallam, Tony. *Catastrophes and Lesser Calamities: The Causes of Mass Extinctions.* Oxford: Oxford University Press, 2004.

Hartmann, William K. and Ron Miller. *The History of the Earth.* New York: Workman Publishing, 1991.

Hunter, Robert. *2030: Confronting Thermageddon in Our Lifetime.* Toronto: McClelland and Stewart, 2002.

Irwin, Douglas H. *Extinction: How Life on Earth Nearly Ended 250 Million Years Ago.* Princeton, New Jersey: Princeton University Press, 2006.

Jacobs, Jane. *The Nature of Economies.* Toronto: Vintage, 2001.

Joseph, Lawrence E. *Gaia: The Growth of an Idea.* New York: St. Martin's Press, 1990.

Knoll, Andrew H. *Life on a Young Planet: The First Three Billion Years of the Evolution on Earth*. Princeton, New Jersey: Princeton University Press, 2003.

Lane, Nick. *Oxygen: The Molecule that Made the World*. Oxford: Oxford University Press, 2002.

Leggett, Jeremy. *Global Warming: The Greenpeace Report*. Oxford: Oxford University Press, 1990.

Lesley, John. *The End of the World: The Science and Ethics of Human Extinction*. London: Routledge, 1996.

Lovelock, James. *The Ages of Gaia: A Biography of Our Living Earth*. Toronto: Penguin Books, 1988.

McDonough, William and Michael Braungart. *Cradle to Cradle: Remaking the Way We Make Things*. New York: North Point Press, 2002.

Macdougall, Doug. *Frozen Earth: The Once and Future Story of the Ice Ages*. Berkeley, California: University of California Press, 1994.

Marsden, William. *Stupid to the Last Drop: How Alberta is Bringing Environmental Armageddon to Canada (And Doesn't Seem to Care)*. Toronto: Alfred A. Knopf, 2007.

McKibben, Bill. *The End of Nature*. New York: Random House, 1989.

Meadows, Donella H., Dennis Meadows, Jorgen Randers and William W. Behrens III. *Limits to Growth: A Report for the Club of Rome's Project on the Predicament of Mankind*. New York: Universe Books, 1974.

Monbiot, George. *Heat: How to Stop the Planet from Burning*. Toronto: Anchor, 2006.

Rathje, William and Cullen Murphy. *Rubbish: The Archeology of Garbage*. New York: HarperCollins Publishers, 1992.

Raup, David M. *Extinction: Bad Genes or Bad Luck*. New York: WW Norton and Company, 1991.

Rees, Martin. *Our Final Hour: A Scientist's Warning*. New York: Basic Books, 2003.

Schneider, Stephen H. *Global Warming: Are We Entering the Greenhouse Century?* New York: Century Vintage Books, 1989.

Simpson, Jeffrey, Mark Jaccard and Nic Rivers. *Hot Air: Meeting Canada's Climate Change Challenge*. Toronto: McClelland and Stewart, 2007.

Stanley, Steven M. *Earth System History*. New York: W.H. Freeman & Co., 1999.

Stanley, Steven M. *Extinction*. New York: Scientific American Library, 1987.

Wilson, Edward O. *The Future of Life*. New York: Vintage Books, Random House, 2002.

Ward, Peter D. and Donald Brownlee. *Life and Death of the Planet Earth*. New York: Henry Holt and Company, 2002.

Ward, Peter D. *The Call of Distant Mammoths: Why the Ice Age Mammals Disappeared*. New York: Copernicus, Springer-Verlag, 1997.

Ward, Peter D. *Rivers in Time: The Search for Clues to the Earth's Mass Extinctions*. New York: Columbia University Press, 2000.

Wise Bauer, Susan. *The History of the Ancient World: From the Earliest Accounts to the Fall of Rome*. New York: WW Norton and Company, 2007.

Wright, Ronald. *A Short History of Progress*. Toronto: House of Anansi Press, 2004.

About the Author

Richard Zurawski is a documentary filmmaker, writer, meteorologist, television and radio host, and public speaker living in Halifax, Nova Scotia, where he has an independent production company, PAL Science Media Inc., and is the on-air meteorologist for Rogers Radio.

His first book was *Richard Zurawski's Book of Maritime Weather*. Richard has also created many documentaries about science, weather and history, as well as producing television series for children about science, weather and mathematics (*The Adventures of the AfterMath Crew* and *WiseWeatherWhys*).

For his documentary productions and research for books, he has travelled around the world, from Iran to India to Australia to Japan. In the coming year he'll be in Ukraine, Mongolia, Syria and the Antarctic for a new series of documentaries and books.

His documentaries air around the world and a short list includes *Mega Storms*, *Rail Against the Machine*, *It Starts with Z: Finding Zarathushtra* and *Moving People*. Currently he is producing a limited three-hour series for Discovery HD and CLT called *M5 – Mighty, Mega, Monster, Medieval Machines*.

He can be heard on the Rogers Maritime Radio Group (95.7 in Halifax, 91.9 in Moncton and 88.9 in Saint John) five days a week, Monday to Friday, forecasting the weather for the Maritimes and doing the Science Files on Fridays with Andrew Krystal from 11 a.m. to noon (Atlantic time). You can catch the broadcasts on the Web as well. Richard also has a blog on his website (www.richardzurawski.ca).